GOURDON:

A BRIEF HISTORY
OF
THE VILLAGE AND ITS PEOPLE

1500-1800

by

ANDREW R. C. SIMPSON

Copyright 2005 Aberdeen & North-East Scotland Family History Society

(www.anesfhs.org.uk)

ISBN:

1-900173-98-0
978-1-900173-98-8

First published November 2005
Reprinted 2011

Published by
Aberdeen & North-East Scotland Family History Society

Printed by
McKenzie Quality Print Ltd.,, Howe Moss Crescent, Kirkhill Industrial Estate, Dyce, Aberdeen
AB21 0GN

DEDICATION

*This book is dedicated to the memory of three sisters,
Anne Gowan, wife of Alexander Moncur, Margaret Gowan, wife
of Joseph Craig, and May Gowan, wife of Andrew Lownie. Without their
wonderful memories, inspiring stories and natural ability to bring
history back to life, this history could never have been written.*

*This book is further dedicated to the memory of Mrs Annie Gowans Pittock,
nee Mowat, whose stories inspired this work. I hope that this history will
help them to live on.*

Anne Gowan (1845-1928), wife of Alexander Moncur

CONTENTS

CHAPTER/PART   *PAGE*

Dedication   iii

Acknowledgements   vi

List of Photographs   vii

Introduction   viii

One   **The Village**   1

Two   **The Families**   9

Three   **Fishing, Trade and the Sea**   21

Four   **The Kirk and the Village**   38

Five   **Gourdon and the Law**   63

Conclusion   75

Bibliography   78

Appendix 1 – Gourdon Wills (pre-1800)   81
Appendix 2 – Neglected Bervie Christenings (1660s)   84
Appendix 3 – List of Inhabitants of Benholm, mid 1600s   86
Appendix 4 – Rental of Hallgreen (1769)   89
Appendix 5 – Constructing the Gowan Line   92
Appendix 6 – Lineage of the Author   96

Index of Persons   98

ACKNOWLEDGEMENTS

First of all, I would like to thank two of the historians of Gourdon – Robert Gove and Roy Souter – for all of their help in providing me with large amounts of information on the subject of the history of the village, and for the ongoing encouragement they gave me to continue in my own researches. Without their help, and the work of the late Robert Gowans of Gourdon, who was the first man to write down the history of the village in any detail, along with the irreplaceable oral traditions of his great-aunts, Anne, Margaret and May Gowan, it would have been considerably more difficult, if not impossible, for me to piece together much of this history. I also wish to thank Professor Devine of the Research Institute of Irish and Scottish Studies for his kind words and encouragement with regard to the work. Various other members of the family and some other friends have encouraged and helped me greatly in my researches, including the late Annie Pittock (nee Mowatt), Isles Burness, John Ritchie, Allistair Pullar, Iain Watt, and Elinor Christie, my aunt, and for this help I also extend my thanks. Furthermore, I wish to acknowledge all the help given to me by the staff at Angus Archives, the National Archives of Scotland, Aberdeen City Archives, the Aberdeen and North East of Scotland Family History Society, Aberdeen Central Library, Inverbervie Library, Dundee Central Library, Dundee City Archives, the Tay Valley Family History Society, Stonehaven Library and Edinburgh City Archives. Without the help of the staff at each of these locations, I would not have got very far. In this respect, mention should go in particular to the staff at Angus Archives – namely Fiona Scharlau, Heather Munro, Ruth Parsonson and Sheila Simpson. It should be noted, however, that any errors in the work remain entirely my own.

The author and publisher have made every effort to contact copyright holders whose work is included in this book; however, omissions may inadvertently have occurred, and they will be pleased to hear from any copyright holder whose work is not properly acknowledged.

LIST OF PHOTOGRAPHS

vii

1. The village of Gourdon today

2. Old Gourdon looking towards Craig David

3. "The Hill" overlooking Gourdon Harbour

4. Ruins of Old Bervie Kirk

5. Headstone in Bervie Kirkyard

6. Lang Close and Shore Inn

7. Probable site of the Slough of Despond

8. Mowatt's Lane

9. The (probable) Hawyning Place of Gerdoun (mentioned 1549)

10. The main harbour today

11. The main harbour today

INTRODUCTION

"As a trait of the character of the people of this parish,
they are by no means addicted to litigation; are too wise to
give their money to lawyers, and neither plague their heads
with politics nor religion."

Thus, in 1792, Walter Thom, a manufacturer who was later to be the captain of the local militia during the Napoleonic Wars, summed up his understanding of the character of the people of the parish of Inverbervie, in Kincardineshire. He gives an image of a rather docile community – a place where the people seemed to be somewhat anaesthetised in relation to the political and religious troubles of the day. More than that, his understanding of the people was that they considered themselves quite able to manage their disputes in such a way as to avoid what was sometimes referred to as the *"demon of litigation."* Other communities might have troublemakers; the parish of Bervie did not.

At the southern edge of this parish lies the village of Gourdon, a community of one hundred and eighty-eight people in Thom's day. The villagers to this day have very strong traditions about their roots, which lie in the people described above by Thom. These traditions give a somewhat more colourful view of the people of the village than that painted by Thom. Descendants of the people of Gourdon, like myself, today look back to ancestors who were fishers and smugglers, with lives that were financially on a knife-edge between prosperity and poverty, always at the mercy of the sea. These traditions paint a picture of poor people, but not really of docile people. One tradition notes that, when need was at its greatest, the villagers were not above rioting if faced with potential starvation caused by the high price of meal. There are also some very strong traditions in relation to some of the more religious members of the community – but by and large these traditions pertain to people who lived after 1800, like Anne Gowan (Mrs. Moncur), who was a deeply committed Christian. The Christian faith of many of the villagers by the nineteenth century was very much one of the defining characteristics of the people. But traditions in the earlier period are much more hazy; John Wesley preached on Knox's Hill; and an early tradition mentions a visit by the minister to the village. In this story, the minister was introduced to one of the children of the man he had gone to visit; and, having asked the man what the child's name was, the man scratched his head, turned towards his wife, and enquired, *"Ann, whit's Pedlar's richt name?"* The man had become so used to using the child's by-name that he had forgotten his real name!

There is some discrepancy, then, between the traditions and Thom's account, as to the true character of the people of Gourdon. Naturally one cannot truly say that there was ever a uniform character possessed by the villagers; but the discrepancy does beg a question – can we look back into that community, which has now been gone for over two hundred years, to discern something of the character of the people of Gourdon? The researcher in this area is instantly confronted by difficulties. Records generally concentrate on the extraordinary and on negative brushes with the law. Customs records can tell us something about smuggling; but they will never tell us the full extent or the success of these ventures, or what we can truly tell about the character of the people from this activity – we must look further for that. Kirk Session records are of some use in showing whether or not the kirk approved of certain individuals; but we must always remember that these records were not kept to record the good that people did within their communities – rather to record their misdemeanours. So any assessment of the strength of the Christian faith in the village in this period is hampered by the fact that the primary source on this point is, by its nature, one-sided. Court processes are, in some ways, the most useful sources of all, for there we can actually discern the voices of some of the villagers themselves, in their pleadings in relation to the disputes in which they found themselves. And there is another, major difficulty – some families in the village are much better documented than others. As regards the traditions themselves, while, of course, one must always be careful in their use as historical sources, it shall be shown that there is, indeed, good reason to think that their collective tenor is true.

In spite of all these difficulties in relation to the reconstruction of the community and its character, I hope to be able to utilise the surviving evidence to paint the true picture of the villagers in the eighteenth century. Naturally this involves the examination of the roots of the village itself, in the sixteenth century and earlier; and the origins of some of the families who lived in Gourdon in the seventeenth century. These issues shall occupy the first two chapters of this study. Following this it is easiest to assess the surviving evidence pertaining to the lives of the villagers by taking in turn each of the major sources of information available to us – the records relating to smuggling and fishing, followed by the Kirk Session records, followed by examples of court processes relating to disputes involving the villagers. At the end of these stages of investigation an attempt will be made to make broad conclusions as to the nature and character of the people of the village in this period. It shall be argued that Thom's assessment of the character of the people of Gourdon is wholly inadequate.

The story of Gourdon is truly fascinating. It makes one appreciate that, however much knowledge of the lives of the villagers has been lost, they lived lives as complex and as full as the lives that we live today.

Andrew R. C. Simpson

Note: It should also be noted that the name "Gowan" was spelt in various ways in the documents, sometimes with an "s" on the end, and sometimes without. The name is spelt in this work in reflection of its spelling in the documents.

CHAPTER ONE:
THE VILLAGE

*"This village is situated on the south corner of the parish
[Bervie] It consists of forty-two habitable houses, besides stables,
barns and granaries. There is a harbour, but it is neither commodious
nor safe."*[1]

Thus began the comments of Walter Thom regarding the small fishing port of Gourdon in Bervie Parish. By his time, in 1792, one hundred and eighty-eight people lived in the forty-two houses of the village,[2] a place set to grow dramatically as the nineteenth century dawned.[3]

But this history does not aim to deal with this later period in the story of the village, but rather to look further back in time, to reconstruct the characters of the villagers in the previous centuries. To do this it is first necessary to examine their changing world – the history of the actual village – and then to examine where these people had their origins. Only then, with this "foundation" of understanding, can each individual's life be properly placed into context.

The origins of Gourdon, like so many subjects of study in early Scottish history, are shrouded in *"thick Cimmerian darkness."*[4] Debate abounds even about the origins of the name itself. There are five main theories. The first, and perhaps most plausible, theory is that the old pronunciation of "Gurden," was taken straight from the original derivation of Gardun, which in Gaelic means "Heron Hill." The prominence of "the Hill" in local folklore would seem to support this, this "Hill" having been the one immediately to the south-west of the present-day village, of which the brae at Gourdon is a continuation.[5] By this the "correct" pronunciation – Gourdon – is actually a corruption, possibly brought in, so it has been said, by French visitors who came to the village.[6] (Naturally such an argument depends upon the French visitors having had a rather strong influence on local pronunciation, and since I find this rather unlikely I am somewhat sceptical about the suggestion – but would be happy to be proved wrong.) What is known is that in 1549 some pronounced the first syllable of the name "Gour."[7]

The other theories as to the origin of the name are equally interesting, but in my opinion the first seems to carry the most compelling argument. One such theory is that the name means "An Arm," "Great Fort," or "Great Hill."[8] It has even been suggested that the name derived from one of the local tribes – the Ma Girghinn. This

---

[1] W. Thom, *Parish of Inverbervie or Bervie*, in Sir John Sinclair (ed.) *Old Statistical Account of Scotland*, Volume XIV – Kincardineshire and South and West Aberdeenshire (1982 reprint) 136-147 at 141

[2] W. Thom, *Op. cit.*, 136-147 at 141; 145

[3] R. Gove, *Gourdon in the Nineteenth Century*, (1980s) (An historical pamphlet published locally based on a talk given by Mr. Gove)

[4] G. Neilson, *Juridicial Review*, III. 12, as cited in T. M. Cooper, *Regiam Majestatem and Quoniam Attachiamenta* (1947) Stair Society Vol. 11 p. 1. (Here the subject of study was somewhat different, being *Regiam Majestatem*, the early work of Scots Law.)

[5] For the identification of the hill to the south of the village as "The hill" I am indebted to the late Annie Gowans Pittock (maiden surname Mowat).

[6] *Ibid*

[7] National Archives of Scotland (NAS) Ref. RH15/37/8

[8] R. Gove, *Op. cit.*

was a Pictish Tribe of the Mearns.[9] All of these are possible derivations of the name, but Gardun makes a considerable amount of sense and explains the old pronunciation.

Whatever the truth of the origin of the name, it is clear that the area has been inhabited for a remarkably long time. The "Werewolf Cairn," near the village, was opened up several decades ago by the Aberdeen Antiquarian Society, and it was found that it was a kitchen midden dating from prehistoric times. Robert Gowans suggested that the old Gourdon Harbour might well have been where these early people fished from, as well as having small farms in the area.[10]

Over time, of course, two distinct communities emerged – the fisher folk and the farm folk of Gourdon.[11] Hence, in 1315, there is a charter mentioning the *"Ferm and Fishertoon of Gurden."*[12] It is, of course, the fishing community that this history is concerned with; there were several other families, such as the Jaffrays, who inhabited the various farms that constituted the farmlands of Gourdon, including the Cauldwell Farm. There was a very long dispute over these farms between Viscount Arbuthnott and Rait of Hallgreen.[13] But it seems that at the earliest known time, the farm town and the fisher town were probably included in the lands of Sillieflat, owned by the Lairds of Hallgreen. From the fifteenth century onwards, these Lairds were the Rait family.[14] They were to play a decisive role in the history of the fishing community of Gourdon.

At this early time, very little is known of the village of Gourdon. There is no known reference to it during the fifteenth century, and it would appear that there was little change in the lives of the villagers at this time. However, one thing about the village can be ascertained at this time – its location.

According to Margaret Gowans (wife of Joseph Craig and my great great grandmother), "Gurden started alang at the Canons."[15] This village has been referred to in later times as the village of Mudlin's Den. According to Robert Gove, it was situated about two hundred yards south of Hallgreen Castle. It was served by a small harbour, but, as was observed by Rait of Hallgreen's lawyer in 1696, it was "useless and unfitt for the statione and safety of boattes."[16] The lawyer simply knew it as the "old port of Gerdonne," and by his day it would appear to have been out of use.

Looking at the site of the old port today, it is fairly clear that only the smallest of fishing boats could have used it. And so one might think it would have remained, were it not the case that, in 1506, there is a rather astonishing piece of history that was uncovered by Robert Gove.[17] At this time, mention was made of the export of wool, hides, salmon and salt fish from Gourdon. This suggests that there were trading ships coming into the village of Gourdon in the reign of James IV. The question, then, is how it was possible for it to be convenient for ships to be exporting from such a small harbour, "useless and unfitt for the statione and safety of boattes," on a regular basis?

---

[9] R. Gowans, *The Gowans*, (1940s) in R. Souter (ed.) *Gourdon and the Surrounding Area – A Compilation of Information and Essays on Local History (unpublished).* For want of a title to the original compilation of essays, I have referred to Mr. Souter's work, which he was kind enough to allow me to inspect, thus.

[10] *Ibid*

[11] As will become apparent, this history focuses to a large extent on the fisher folk of the village.

[12] R. Gove, *Op. cit.*

[13] NAS Ref. RH15/37/133

[14] http://www.geo.ed.ac.uk/scotgaz/towns/townfirst175.html

[15] R. Gowans, *Op. cit.*

[16] NAS Ref. RH15/37/133

[17] R. Gove, *Op. cit.*

The most likely answer to this is that, already, the new harbour of Gourdon had been established at the much more convenient location where the village is today. This was a bigger harbour, much more capable of being accessible to sloops and other such trading vessels. It must be admitted that placing the beginning of the move at this date from Old Gourdon to New Gourdon is entirely theoretical, but there is compelling evidence to support the notion.

One of these pieces of evidence is that it was about this time that more documentation starts to appear in relation to the village in the papers of Rait of Hallgreen. The lairds seem to have been investing in the village, as in 1549, when David Rait of Drumnagair built a Girnel House, possibly the precursor of the Shore Inn at Gourdon.[18] While no description survives of it, it is the first glimpse that we have of the actual buildings in the village itself. By this time there must have been a steady flow of people who were frequenting the Girnel House, as the tenant was the Laird's own son, John Rait. Clearly the Laird would have wanted a good living for him; had the Shore Inn been situated along at the old community, there would have been less scope for the custom of passing merchants.

So by the 1540s Gourdon would seem to have been a developing community, and much of this development (if not all of it) was down to the Rait family of Hallgreen. What is truly fascinating here is the very early presence, characteristic of the Lairds in the Mearns, of an "improving" mentality. They were, in a very primitive way, beginning the process of developing their estates for profit, some considerable time before such changes and improvements are generally thought to have begun. While of course such changes as there were were intermittent and sparse it does seem to imply that the roots of the improving mentality lay, at least in this example, much further back in time than is given credit for. Naturally there is not a vast amount that should be read into this point; there is little conclusive proof as to the motivations that caused these changes, but it is an intriguing hypothesis that in the early 1500s the Raits were improving their estate.

So it is likely that New Gourdon was well under way by the late sixteenth century. This is not to say, however, that the old community did not carry on at the same time as Old Gourdon. It would appear, from oral tradition, that the Mudlin's Den community still existed at the time of one of the most celebrated traditions of Gourdon, spoken of by Margaret Gowan, wife of Joseph Craig, and recorded by Robert Gowans, author of the Gowan family history[19] (the Gowans being one of the larger Gourdon families). It recounts, in 1588, the sinking of one of the retreating ships of the Spanish Armada. According to the story, the people of **Old Gourdon** had been woken one terrible night by the storm, and had gone out of their homes, and seeing five ships of the Armada heading north again in a south-westerly gale, made for the braehead to watch. In an amazingly detailed account (amazing due to the fact that the story, if it is correct, endured for three and a half centuries without being committed to writing) Margaret Gowan told the tale thus:

> "*She was a wounded ane and there was water in her! She*
> *wisna steerin'! They thoucht she wis tryin' to come to the land.*
> *She broached wi' her heid as she came to the shore an' foonderit.*
> *The next day the boats got to sea and brocht in ane or twa bodies*
> *to lat fowk see them. They had awfae bonny claes on. They were*

---

[18] NAS Ref. RH15/37/8

[19] For want of a known title for the original work (which actually consisted of a collection of notes) the *corpus* of notes is referred to here as *The Gowans* (see fn. 9 *supra*).

buriet in Bervie. The ship sank about the Black Ness. "[20]

Of the five ships, it was the "innermost and hindmost of the five"[21] that sank. Such stories of the Spanish Armada are not uncommon in the fishing villages of Scotland, a reminder of the fact that many Spaniards died as they desperately tried to get home after their disastrous military defeat. Some might, justifiably, argue that it is difficult to be certain of the truth behind such an old tradition, dating, as it were, from the late-sixteenth century. It is true that the tradition does carry with it rather a large amount of detail, which might suggest that there is truth in it; I must admit that I am of the view that there is probably some truth in the story. Whatever, it is possible that this is the oldest of the Gourdon traditions.

Old Gourdon was rapidly facing extinction itself. New Gourdon was growing fast; by 1588, there was mention of a breakwater, storehouses and an inn there (possibly the same as the 1549 Girnel House). It is unclear as to when exactly the old village was abandoned; it seems to have been derelict by 1696,[22] but it may have been that by 1641 Old Gourdon was no longer inhabited – the Session Clerk made no distinction between "Old" and "New" Gourdon in the OPRs.[23] This would **suggest** that the old village was finally abandoned in the fifty years after 1588.

But while Old Gourdon was disappearing, New Gourdon was thriving. It was attracting new inhabitants (see Chapter Two), and although no population statistics are available from the seventeenth century, there were at least half a dozen families present by the mid-seventeenth century, of varying sizes. Therefore there must have been a reasonable number of houses in the village by then. These houses were probably in rows, with the gables backing on to the sea, as in other villages and towns of the time. Little is known about these houses at this time (apart from the fact that they were probably quite basic). Stone had clearly been in use in building in the village since 1650, when the Shore Inn was built, and so it is likely that the houses of the village would have been similarly built of stone, by the Laird of Hallgreen.

However, one thing is known about Gourdon as a village in this period, and that is that the Shore Inn was rebuilt. There is no known reason why the old Inn was pulled down, but it was, and it was replaced with a two-storey building that stood until the 1930s. This Shore Inn stood, possibly at the same place as the old Shore Inn (see Chapter Three Section Two), on the one street in the village – the Shorehead, beside the Monument today.[24]

In truth, however, very little is known about the physical appearance of the village until the later eighteenth century. The harbour itself was originally called the "poolie," and the boats were hauled up on to the shore by the houses when not in use. As to the boats themselves, sloops are mentioned in the traditions very early[25] – in 1730 – but apart from that, it would seem that there were a few large fishing craft as well. One of these, which was lost in 1730 in the Storm of Wind,[26] had a crew of nine. The boats and the fishing methods probably employed by the fishermen are discussed further in Chapter Three Section One.[27]

---

[20] R. Gowans, *Op. cit.*

[21] R. Gowans, *Op. cit.*

[22] NAS Ref. RH15/37/133

[23] Inverbervie Old Parish Registers NAS Ref. RD 254 (hereafter Bervie OPRs)

[24] R. Gowans, *Op. cit.*

[25] R. Gowans, *Op. cit.*

[26] Bervie OPRs NAS Ref. RD 254

[27] In Montrose Museum there is a collection of papers that refers to merchant shipping in the Montrose area. One of these papers seems to be a copy of a survey taken immediately after the Union (i.e. in

By the late eighteenth century, a clearer picture of the village emerges from the records. Needless to say, since the Shore Inn was knocked down it is unlikely that old Robert Gowan (one of the Gourdon worthies who shall be referred to throughout this history) or his wife Ann Criggie would have recognised much of the village today. By the time they were in their sixties, in the 1790s, it still remained the case that there was just the one street in the village – the Shorehead.[28] The village had at least extended to the north to where Mowatt's Lane is today, where James Mowat made his home in the 1760s. Again, the houses were probably fairly small, built out of stone and simply furnished. Sadly the surviving wills of the fishers of Gourdon are not detailed enough to give any glimpse of the furnishings of their houses; here and there there is reference to utensils used, such as the jug that was thrown at one of the Customs Officers in the 1770s.[29] It would seem likely that some of the wealthier shipmasters, like James Gowan (d. 1800)[30] might have had a Bible, a fairly common feature of Scottish households of the time, in a land where literacy levels were fairly high. Each of the shipmasters would probably have had some papers as well, in particular if they owned their boats, relating to their trading activities. Most people would have had some sort of lease of their houses from the Laird of Hallgreen, especially those who had the feu of their home.[31] Codlin' Rob, one of the more eccentric descendants of the Gowans, used to keep an old sword at the foot of his bed,[32] perhaps a reminder of times when the Press Gang would come for the fishermen without warning. Perhaps, then, some form of weaponry was present in some of the houses as well. Naturally there would have been some place to put the clothes of the people in the house. Part of the dress for women apparently was "head cloathes."[33] There is no description from the records that survive of the clothes worn by the men of Gourdon, but there was probably some sort of plaid in the earlier days that was worn by them, as by the farm folk, and possibly after one James Mowat set up business in the village as the weaver it was from him that they obtained most of their clothes (see Chapters Four and Five). There is some suggestion that some of the women in the village even wore shoes, (although this is by no means even remotely conclusive) as one of the women was asked, as part of her penance after breaching Kirk Discipline, to appear before the congregation "bare-headed and **bare-footed**."[34]

So, stepping back two centuries, one can almost imagine entering Robert Gowan's home, stooping under a low door, low to keep the heat in. One can picture old Robert Gowan, sitting next to his fire-place in his home, an old man in his sixties, the smoke of the coal fire and odour of fish penetrating every corner of the room and every crease of his clothes. Near him would have been his papers, perhaps with some navigational instruments, and his Bible, possibly stored on a shelf on the wall. In the same room would have been his wife, Ann Criggie,[35] and his younger sons, Alexander and James, with their servant, Margaret Criggie,[36] the latter perhaps helping to

---

1707) for taxation purposes. Here there is reference to a much smaller ship called the *Robert* of Gourdon. This is the first named vessel in the history of Gourdon to which reference has so far been uncovered.

[28] R. Gove, *Op. cit.*

[29] CE53/1/9

[30] NAS Ref. CC20/4/8

[31] NAS Ref. SC5/76/29

[32] Tradition recalled by Duncan Craig Christie (1904 – 1972)

[33] NAS Ref. SC5/8/93

[34] *Ibid*

[35] Bervie OPRs NAS Ref. RD 254; NAS Ref. CH2/34/1

[36] NAS Ref. CH2/34/2

prepare the meal. In the corner, a sword might have guarded the room, opposite some of the everyday utensils that the family used. From hooks on the wall, like those that can still be seen at Crawton, to the north of Gourdon, might have hung various pieces of fishing equipment, and baskets, ready for Ann Criggie to carry, laden with fish, to the market at Bervie or to the Cross at Montrose. Over the fire, a copper kettle would have been beginning to boil, adding steam to the smoke-filled, fish-filled air.

Stepping outside, a visitor to Gourdon would have been greeted by the notorious Slough of Despond[37] – the apt nickname for the village midden, which stretched from the foot of Bridge Street in the present-day village along the Shorehead to the Clover Yard. According to Margaret Gowan, it was filled with the rubbish of the villagers and long, coarse grass grew in it. At one time, a burn ran through it, but it has long since disappeared.[38]

Robert Gowan probably lived in the Lang Close, due to the fact that tradition holds that that was where the family lived.[39] If this were the case, the gable of the block of houses his home was in would have looked out on the sea. Beyond it stretched several more such blocks, clinging to the shore edge, and the Shore Inn, where tradition has it his father had been keeper in the mid-eighteenth century.[40] He seems to have died a fairly comfortable man as he also leased another house in the village from the Barclay-Allardices and sub-let it to one Andrew Jamie.[41]

As the only building of a substantial size in the village until 1819 (it was two stories high) the Shore Inn deserves some attention here. The history of the building itself is patchy at best. It was built in about 1650,[42] probably by Rait of Hallgreen, and probably to replace the older building that served the same purpose. It survived almost three hundred years, until it was pulled down in the 1930s, along with most of the houses in the Lang Close.[43] Some photographic evidence survives about it, showing that it had a single window on the second storey that faced out to sea. Apart from a few other references to it, however – such as that involving an old sailor called Alexander Gowan who lived there, was "dottled" and "steered with the bed rail all night"[44] – there is little to say about the Inn directly. However, judging by its size and date of construction, we might be able to draw a comparison between it and a remarkably well preserved historic building of the time – Hugh Miller's Cottage, in Cromarty. This National Trust for Scotland property is one that really helps us to gain a picture of the old Shore Inn.

Hugh Miller's cottage was built in the first years of the eighteenth century, about fifty years after the Shore Inn. According to the National Trust Booklet[45] on the subject, the cottage:

*"was constructed with locally collected red sandstone, compacted
with mud and straw. There are no foundations and originally the floors
would have been bare, hardened clay, kept clean with
strewings of sand or straw."*[46]

---

[37] R. Gowans, *Op. cit.*; R. Gove, *Op. cit.*

[38] R. Gowans, *Op. cit.*

[39] *Ibid*

[40] *Ibid*

[41] *Gowans v Jeamie* NAS Ref. SC5/8/132

[42] R. Gove, *Op. cit.*

[43] R. Gowans, *Op. cit.*

[44] *Ibid*

[45] M. and F. Gostwick, *Hugh Miller's Cottage* (NTS Publication, available at the property in question)

[46] *Ibid*, p. 8

This description is perhaps close to how the Shore Inn would have appeared. The two buildings would seem to have been of about the same size, produced by the same sort of community and lived in by the same sort of people – traders and fishers. Both had two stories, and several rooms. Miller's cottage had a thatched roof; perhaps originally the Shore Inn, and indeed other buildings in the village, did as well. The small, single window facing the sea was so designed to minimise the force of the elements on the building. There was also a fireplace in the Shore Inn, set into the wall facing the sea, as shown by a chimney that appears on a photo of the Shore Inn dating from 1911. Around this might have been a few chairs, still the centre-point of the room while the people endured the freezing winter evenings, and above it a copper kettle, or a pot for cooking.[47] Apart from this, much of the interior would have resembled a larger version of the home of Robert Gowan, with the probable description thereof included above. A crucial difference, however, is that in the Shore Inn there would have been a large supply of alcohol, and there is tradition that grog was imported from Holland for the place, and there is further mention of brandy and ale in the records being consumed in the village.[48]

One interesting and final point to note on this subject is that Miller's cottage had a garden;[49] in the case of the Shore Inn, there is no evidence either way on this point. One might imagine a small strip of land behind the building where vegetables would have been grown.

There were other buildings in the village, including several "victual houses,"[50] most of which belonged to one or other of the Lairds. They were simply storehouses; there is no evidence that the people bought food from them. Until the nineteenth century, there were no shops or even a village school;[51] the buildings in the village were connected either with fishing and trade or with habitation. (It should be noted that Thom also mentions stables in the village.[52]) Due to the lack of shops, food was obtained either, as is obvious, from the sea, or possibly from small vegetable gardens, although there is no mention that such things existed. It is more likely that the country people bartered with the fisherfolk, exchanging fish for agricultural produce, giving the villagers more of a balance in their diet. Failing this, the markets at Bervie or at Montrose were always options. Water was obtained, as Robert Gove has pointed out, from "privately owned" wells by the houses or from the communal "Cauldwell."[53]

Beyond the village itself, the villagers claimed certain rights to the rocks on the shore to the north and south, in particular to gather kelp. Robert Gowans mentions two examples of these claims – two "sloughs," where the kelp was gathered – those of "Mary Bang" and "Jean Ravel"! Their names give a wonderful indication of their characters.[54]

Therefore, in brief, the basic background to the history of the physical buildings of the village has been demonstrated in this chapter. Naturally, there is much more that could have been said, and archaeological digs in certain parts of the

---

[47] Based on a visit to the cottage 31/8/2002
[48] CE53/1/9
[49] M. and F. Gostwick, *Op. cit.,* p. 15
[50] W. Thom. *Op. cit.* at 141-143
[51] R. Gove, *Op. cit.*
[52] W. Thom, *Op. cit.* at 141
[53] R. Gove, *Op. cit.*
[54] R. Gowans, *Op. cit.*

village would probably enrich enormously this description. Much of this description has been based on some degree of speculation, in particular with regard to dating the move from Old Gourdon to New Gourdon. Having examined the origins and skeleton history of the village itself, in the next chapter the origins of some of the villagers will be traced.

Whatever the truth behind many of these speculations about the past of Gourdon, they are part of a truly fascinating tale. It is a tale that takes on new dimensions at each turn, looking into many of the most important aspects of Scottish society at the time, with regards to the Kirk, the Law, trade and fishing. These first two chapters are the stage-set for a veritable historical drama.

CHAPTER TWO:
THE FAMILIES

It is little exaggeration to say that the people of Gourdon were all related to one another, either by, as was usually the case, kin, or at least by kith. The various families could all point to distant patriarchs, and while there may not have been twelve tribes, there certainly were some vast families. The purpose of this brief section is to describe the background of some of the Gourdon families in the period – particularly the Gowans, the Jeamies (or Jamies), the Mearns family and the Ritchies or, as they also seem to have been known, the Fatts. The aim here is to provide the necessary background knowledge to facilitate the reader's understanding of the histories of these families as this book continues to discuss the (predominantly eighteenth century) history of the family.

Part One: The Earliest Families

Gourdon has been inhabited for centuries,[55] but the first named villager was John Rait, son of the Laird of Hallgreen, who was the Tacksman of the Laird's Girnel House in 1549.[56] The records do not allow us to conclude that he left descendants in Gourdon. Nonetheless, it is with him that we see the beginning of the recorded history of the people of Gourdon.

The oldest Gourdon families who were fishing families were the Todds, the Mearns family, the Ritchies and the Jeamies. The Spences perhaps arrived in the early seventeenth century, and possibly played a crucial role in the history of the village. Their impact is discussed in the section regarding the history of the in-comer families to the village (see *Part Two* below).

The names of these families are of some help in identifying their earliest origins. The simplest name to understand is that of Mearns – this family descended in the male line from people who originated in the county of the Mearns.[57] According to Black, the first of this name (of whom record has survived) appeared in 1401 in Aberdeen.[58] However, it has to be borne in mind that not all those bearing the name Mearns necessarily share a common ancestor. Two unrelated families could take the same habitational surname.

The first known person to have the name in Gourdon was Andrew Mearns, who was found guilty of theft in 1618 (see Chapter Five) along with David Todd.[59] Both were probably born in the latter years of the sixteenth century, and they are the first named inhabitants of the village who were fishermen. Although it is now impossible to ascribe to either of these individuals an exact relationship to those of the name that followed them, it would seem plausible that some of the subsequent Mearnses of Gourdon (the word "some" being important here as the name was very common in the coastal communities throughout the county) were connected to old Andrew Mearns.

The family continued to grow throughout the seventeenth century, and by 1648 two of them appeared on the Poor Roll – David Meirnes and Issobell Mearns.[60]

---

[55] R. Gove, *Gourdon in the Nineteenth Century* (1980s)
[56] NAS Ref. RH15/37/8
[57] G. F. Black, *The Surnames of Scotland* (1946) at 590 (1999 edition)
[58] *Ibid*
[59] R. Gove, *Op. cit.*
[60] NAS Ref. CH2/34/9

They may have belonged to the same generation as Andrew Mearns **if** they were on poor relief due to advanced age and the resulting inability to work. This is purely speculative, however.

In the village there were probably later Mearnses who were not directly connected to the older Gourdon family. It is possible that some (if not all) were connected to the Mearns family of Johnshaven, of whom three males appear in the listing of Johnshaven inhabitants in the early seventeenth century (see Appendix Three). It seems likely that Robert Mearns, who may have been the husband of one Agnes Gowan, did not hail directly from the old Gourdon family.[61] The families came and went, and those like the Gowans and the Jeamies, who remained steadfastly in Gourdon, were not necessarily typical of all of the families in the village. (The evidence does not support multiple families of Gowans in the village.)

The highly obscure Todd family of Gourdon was also one of the oldest families in the village. Their name, according to Black, comes from the word "fox," and refers to the character of the original bearer. The first recorded Gourdon Todd was David Todd (see above) in 1618. Another David Tod appears in 1648, on the Bervie Poor Roll,[62] but the name was dwindling even at this early stage. There was one John Tod in Johnshaven in the early 1600s[63] as well, but the name seems to have largely disappeared from Gourdon by the early eighteenth century. Gowans makes no mention of them in his history of the Gowan family,[64] and it would appear that they had been largely forgotten until Robert Gove uncovered the court case involving one of them.

One of the more confusing of the Gourdon families, in that they sometimes used an alias, was the Ritchie family, who, according to an old tradition recorded by Roy Souter, were also known as the Fatts (the *"Fatt family later changed their name to Ritchie."*)[65] Is this correct? From the surviving OPRs for Bervie, I think it is absolutely clear that the name change did occur. For example, in the seventeenth century, Margarit Richie was christened on 28th March 1675, the daughter of David Richie and Margarit Jamie. She had a brother Thomas, christened on 31st March 1672. So David Richie had two children. But, assuming for the moment that the tradition is correct, he also had two other children. One David Fatt and Margaret Jeamie had a son (whose name is not recorded or has been obliterated from the record) christened on 24th December 1682 in Bervie, and a daughter, Isobella, christened on 4th August 1678 in Bervie. *Prima facie* there is a common denominator – Margaret Jamie with a husband called David. So here are ostensibly two families – the family of David Fatt and Margaret Jamie and the family of David Richie and Margaret Jamie – which, were the tradition concerning the name change correct, could in fact be identified as one family. And this happens at least twice more in the records. Anna Ritchie, daughter of Thomas Ritchie and Anne Alexander, was christened on 6th June 1763 in Benholm. No Thomas Ritchie is on record as having been married to an Anne Alexander, but one Thomas Fatt married an Anne Alexander on June 22nd 1758 in Bervie. Finally, Thomas Richie married Isabel Hay on 29th December 1774. They had a large family of children with the surname Richie. But there was one William Fatt christened on January 6th 1778 son of Thomas Fatt and

---

[61] Kinneff and Catterline OPRs (1696)

[62] NAS Ref. CH2/34/9

[63] NAS Ref. RH15/37/192

[64] R. Gowans, *The Gowans*, in Souter (ed.) *Gourdon and the Surrounding Area – A Compilation of Information and Essays on Local History (unpublished)*

[65] R. Gowans, *Op. cit.*

Isabel Hay. Again, it seems likely that we are not dealing with two separate families here; no Thomas Fatt is on record as having married any Isabel Hay. The conclusion is clear; these three instances point to the veracity of the tradition that the Fatts changed their name to Ritchie. Otherwise we would be dealing with a situation with multiple Richies and Fatts with wives bearing the same names. Furthermore, there is reference to a David Richie alias Fatt in 1668, and a Thomas Richie alias Fatt in 1669, in the list of christenings shown in Appendix Two.[66]

The first reference found to date of either a Ritchie or a Fatt in the area was of William Fatt, who was made a Timberman Burgess of Montrose in 1637.[67] There were two Ritchies in Johnshaven only a few years later, and so the question remains wide open as to what the original name of the family was.

Black makes no mention of the name "Fatt" in his *"Surnames of Scotland,"*[68] and Dorward in his *"Scottish Surnames,"*[69] makes no mention of it either. Clearly, therefore, it was a remarkably obscure surname, which might possibly suggest that Ritchie was actually the original name and that "Fatt" had been given as a nickname to some progenitor of the family. The name "Ritchie" is, of course, well documented, as a diminutive of Richard, the name having a similar origin to the name Jeamie – the family would have been descended from one called Richard.

Once again, this is one of the older families of Gourdon. Due to the presence of William Fatt in Montrose in 1636 there is a possibility that the family may have hailed from there originally, but equally, and more probably, this Fatt came south to Montrose from either Johnshaven or Gourdon, due to the extreme lack of records in the Montrose OPRs at this date concerning them. There was also a Thomas Fatt who appeared in Fetteresso in 1622.[70] He also could have been a progenitor of the Ritchie family of Gourdon.

The Ritchies grew to become one of the more numerous Gourdon families, and were certainly alongside the Gowans and the Jeamies in being very active within the community. Sometimes this was not with the best results; one of the earliest appearances in history of the family was in 1654, when Thomas and David Fatt, one in Gourdon and the other in Johnshaven, were found guilty of "breaking" the head of John Anderson "with a dirk!"[71] The first Ritchies in Gourdon who were recorded in the church records were Thomas Ritchie (who married Margaret Small in 1653[72] and could have been the same individual who was involved in the 1654 incident), Jon Ritchie and Kathren Ritchie (the last two being among those who appear on the 1648 Poor Roll).[73]

These three families were among the more significant known early inhabitants of the village who may have been natives, or who at least were present in the village in the sixteenth century. Of course there were many other names in the village at the time – Nicoll, Cormack and Blews to name but three – but their impact was less on the village, and they were never numerous. However, now some attention must be paid to the in-comer families to the village, as two of them in particular, the Jeamies

---

[66] These dates of birth and dates of marriage are taken from:
http://www.familysearch.org/Eng/Search/frameset_search.asp?PAGE=igi/search_IGI.asp&clear_form=true, the family history website. In turn the information comes from the Bervie and Benholm OPRs.
[67] Montrose Town Council Minutes, Volume One, Transcription (available at Angus Archives).
[68] G. Black, *Op. cit.*
[69] D. Dorward, *Scottish Surnames* (2002)
[70] Fetteresso OPRs
[71] NAS Ref. SC5/1/2
[72] Bervie OPRs
[73] NAS Ref. CH2/34/9

and the Gowans, were to be deeply involved in most of the history of Gourdon, and were to become, by the end of the eighteenth century, among the most numerous, if not the most numerous, families in the village. Their history is fascinating, and also remarkably well documented and recorded.

Part Two: Those from "Ower the Hill"

The term most often used to describe those who were not native to Gourdon was that they were from "ower the hill." Many of the most numerous of the Gourdon families were given this description; Annie Pittock used it to describe the origins of the Gowans, and Liz Lownie of the Lang Close used it to describe the origins of the Lownie family ("the first Lownie cam' ower the hill a' the wye fae Ireland and marret ane o' the Gowans.")[74] The origin of the phrase itself is easy enough to discern – to get to Gourdon a person has to come over a hill and down the brae to the sea-front. This hill, Annie Pittock thought, was probably the hill to the south of the village. It is possible that the term was used in the general fashion, referring to any in-comer, but notably James Mowat, progenitor of the Mowats, who came from north of the village, was never described as being from over the hill. Neither were the Moncurs, who also arrived from the north in the period between 1841 and 1851.[75] It is perhaps too loose a term to speculate on, but it might suggest that it did not refer to those from the northern part of the Mearns.

The account that relates to the first known incomers to Gourdon comes from 1832, now recorded in "Fraser Papers,"[76] that the Earl Marischal and Arbuthnott of Arbuthnott desired very much to improve the village of Gourdon in this period. The story goes that they brought fishermen from other fishing villages to populate their own rapidly growing community. It has long been held that other landowners did the same; in the neighbouring parish of Benholm, the Laird of Brotherton brought fishermen from Peterhead to populate Johnshaven.[77] But, while this is unremarkable, what the account goes on to say is astonishing. It makes the claim that these fishermen were brought from Yorkshire! At first glance the account seems somewhat bizarre, but it does go on to give evidence for this assertion, tracing the distinctive Gourdon "speak" as having traces of Yorkshire dialect in it:

> *"Horse they pronounce ors; head, ide; hand – and; hole, ole;*
> *ox, hox; hen, en."*[78]

Another point to make is that some of the superstitions and traditions in Gourdon bore more similarity to those of the Yorkshire communities than the other Scottish communities. For example, in many Scottish communities it was customary for fishermen to be carried out to their boats by their wives.[79] In stark contrast to this, in Gourdon it was considered unlucky for the womenfolk to see them off – as in Yorkshire.[80] I think that this point is a much stronger basis for the argument that

---

[74] R. Gowans, *Op. cit.*
[75] 1841 Census, Crawton Village, Dunnottar Parish; 1851 Census, Gourdon
[76] W. Fraser, *Papers from the Collection of Sir William Fraser* (1924) at 55
[77] R. Souter, *Op. cit.*
[78] W. Fraser, *Op. cit.*
[79] http://sites.scran.ac.uk/collieston/Themes/Themes.html;
http://www.lossiefowk.co.uk/articles/imlach.htm
[80] http://www.hull.ac.uk/php/cetag/5bseadal.htm

Gourdon had some form of connection with the English county than the linguistic evidence above. Sadly, it now seems impossible to work out who these Yorkshiremen were, but it would seem that it is plausible that they did leave their mark on the history of the village.

In-comer families to the village were always numerous in times past, and many of the names in the village appear and disappear and reappear with regularity. It would be a momentous task indeed to chart the histories of all of these families, and here it is entirely unnecessary. Here it is better to concentrate on the larger in-comer families who did have a major effect on the history of the village, in particular the Jeamies and the Gowan family, along with the Spences.

One of the oldest, most numerous and active of the Gourdon families, the Jeamies, has a very interesting history. The name itself, according to Black,[81] is a diminutive of James, and so it seems likely that some distant ancestor of the family was called James. The first of the Jeamies in Bervie Parish who is known today was William Jeamie. He was not a fisher, but a farmer, and was one of the first inhabitants of the parish to appear on the OPR:

"Upon the auchteen day of August 1641 umqll Wm Jamie in hilsyd and Marie Arbuthnott his spouse had ane son baptised called Wm Wm Napier baillie [of Bervie] *and Wm Arbuthnott son to G[eorge?] Arbuthnott in Sillieflat gossopes"*[82]

This infers that the family was originally among the farm folk of Bervie Parish. Perhaps members of this family went to the sea, perhaps starting off working on the farm of Gourdon and then moving to the village. Interestingly enough, it would seem that William was dead by the time his son was born (he was "umqll"), and so this may have sparked the move from this farm to another, if there was no one in the family who could carry it on. It is dangerous to speculate to too great an extent based on the surviving evidence, but this may have led to some hardship – on the 1648 Bervie Poor Roll, one David Jeamie is mentioned.[83] Certainly there were three Jeamies in the village by the 1660s; there was possibly already one there in 1646, as a Jeamie witnessed the birth of Jon Gowans, son of Jon Gowans, in that year.[84] It should be noted that there was also a family of Jeamies (or "Geimies") in St Cyrus, as shown in Appendix Two, with the marriage of Robert Gemie in Eiglishgrieg to Margaret Watt in Bervie in June 1666.[85] There may be a connection of some sort between the two families.

As stated, the family was both numerous and active throughout the seventeenth and eighteenth centuries. There is no need to go into this here, as their history is discussed throughout the rest of the book. Suffice to say, they were great smugglers, and their lives were as closely bound to the history of the village as any, and there is hardly a document relating to the history of the fisher town of Gourdon that does not refer to them.

The Spence family was in Gourdon from the commencement of the records that have survived that were kept by the Kirk. There are four named Spences in Gourdon – John Spence, his daughter Margaret Spence (who was baptised in 1642),

---

[81] Black, *Op. cit.*, p. 382
[82] Bervie OPRs NAS Ref. RD 254
[83] NAS Ref. CH2/34/9
[84] Bervie OPRs NAS Ref. RD 254
[85] (See Appendix Two)

Margaret Spence (who married Patrick Reid in Benholm in 1668, perhaps the same person) and another female Spence, who was the wife of the first of the Gowans of Gourdon, Jon Gowans, and who is therefore, probably, the matriarch of all the Gowans of Gourdon.[86]

Of the family only John Spence is any more than a mere name to us. His only appearance in any record was in 1642, when his daughter was christened. His wife's name was Margaret Nicoll,[87] and he himself was among the first of the recorded Gourdon shipmasters. The family, while small at the outset, came to be connected by blood or marriage to almost all of the later Gourdon families, as the Gowans were descended from them, and through the Gowans many of the Jeamies, the Ritchies and the Mearnses.

The first tie between the Spences and one of the more familiar Gourdon families appears in the records for 1642. In this year, when Margaret Spence was born, Thomas Fatt was the witness at the christening.[88] This may be the same Thomas Fatt who, twelve years later, was involved with David Fatt in an attack on one of the Johnshaven shipmasters (see Chapter Five). Clearly they were integrated into the community by this date.

The second tie appears in the records of the same year, when, as mentioned above, a female Spence was recorded as the wife of Jon Gowans, first of the Gowans of Gourdon (see the section below on the Gowans). When he was first mentioned in 1642, Gowans was simply described as "in Gourdon," whereas John Spence was a "Skipper in Gourdon." However, four years later, Gowans's designation had changed – he was now the Skipper. There were no further Spences recorded as being born in the village in this period – it seems likely that John Spence was the last of this particular family of Spences (much later on there was another family of that name in the village). It is just possible that he died between 1642 and 1646, and that the boat passed to Jon Gowans, who could easily have been a brother-in-law, or even a son-in-law. This could have been the "making" of the Gowans as a fairly comfortable family, by Gourdon standards. Naturally one must bear in mind that this is extremely difficult to assert with any certainty.

But what of the origins of the Spences themselves? There is almost no evidence about this that has survived. The fact that there were only three of them recorded would suggest that they had not been in Gourdon for very long. Clearly they had come from elsewhere, and had a maritime background, since Spence was the Skipper. There were later Spences in the village, but since for many years no Spences can be found in the records, I believe that the two families were different. It is just possible that they originated in either Brechin (where later Spences were town clerks) or in Montrose, (where a merchant named Spence is recorded in the mid-fifteenth century). In all probability, however, this speculation is as far as any enquiry into the origins of the Spences could go. Whoever they were, the Spences did have an impact on the history of the village, and it still remains in them that we find one of the earliest recorded Gourdon Skippers.

Turning to the Freemans, according to Black, the name of this family comes from the Old English "freo-mann," simply meaning what it says – a free man.[89] The Gourdon family, while not very well documented in the seventeenth century, has certainly been in the parish of Bervie, and possibly Gourdon itself, since 1644, (in

---

[86] Bervie OPRs NAS Ref. RD 254
[87] Bervie OPRs NAS Ref. RD 254
[88] Bervie OPRs NAS Ref. RD 254
[89] Black, *Op. cit.*, p. 279

truth it is not even certain that they were incomers) when one John Fremane stood as a witness for a christening for one of the Gourdon families.[90] Because of the lack of evidence about this earliest recorded Fremane it is difficult to assign to him the designation of "progenitor" of the Freemans of Gourdon. They began to be more numerous after the 1680s, and by the early decades of the eighteenth century, as Gowans observed, they were very numerous indeed. But unlike the Gowans and the Jeamies they seem to have concentrated more on the fishing than on trading. In 1730, this hazardous occupation caused what must have been one of the greatest disasters of all time for the family and the village as a whole – Alexander Freeman lost his boat, his crew and his own life in the infamous "Storm of Wind."[91]

Nonetheless, the Freemans survived such setbacks, and remained one of the more numerous families, to the end of the eighteenth century and beyond. Among their number was one who was at Trafalgar in 1805,[92] showing how involved the family was in the history of the day.

One of the oldest and most numerous of the Gourdon families was the Gowan or Gowans family. This family is without a doubt the best documented of the families of Gourdon. As shall be seen, this is reflected in the extent to which we may say more about their history in comparison to other Gourdon families. This in itself is in no small way also down to the earlier work of Roy Souter and Robert Gove, and in particular Robert Gowans, who first wrote down many of his family's oral traditions.

The name itself comes from the Gaelic "gobhainn," which has its roots in the word "gobha," meaning "smith."[93] (It should be remembered that some still think that the name derives from the word "daisy" as the old Scots word for a daisy was "gowan." However, Black does not consider this as the potential root of the name and so until other evidence is found to the contrary it shall be assumed that he was correct to identify a Gaelic root for the name.) From this it is therefore clear that, in ancient times, the original Gowans were smiths of some sort. The real question surrounding this is as to where they were smiths. My grandfather, Duncan Craig Christie (1904-1972), himself the grandson of Margaret Gowan, wife of Joseph Craig, and so the great great great grandson of Robert Gowan (b. 1731)[94] handed down an old story that the Gowans had some connection to Clan MacDonald. For evidence to support this he pointed to his great-grandmother's plaid, which is in the Ancient MacDonald tartan, and dates to the 1840s. On this is based the theory that there may have been some connection with that vast clan centuries ago. It is the case that the family of MacGowan is a recognised sept of Clan MacDonald,[95] but as yet no proof has been found to link the two up. It should be noted that it is strange that Robert Gowans made no mention of this tradition in his history of the family,[96] but this does not necessarily invalidate what my grandfather said – the sources for their stories were (presumably) the same people, and they may have inherited different strands of the traditions from them.

Whatever the truth of their earliest origins, one thing is certain, and that is that they must have come from a Gaelic-speaking area. Fortunately, however, the records

---

[90] Bervie OPRs NAS Ref. RD 254
[91] Bervie OPRs NAS Ref. RD 254
[92] Newspaper article formerly in the keeping of Mrs Annie Pittock or Mowat
[93] Black, *Op. cit.*, p. 322
[94] Bervie OPRs; NAS Ref. RD 245 Statutory Records; Census Returns for Gourdon 1841-1891; R. Gowans, *Op. cit.*
[95] See, for example, http://www.electricscotland.com/webclans/m/macdona.html
[96] R. Gowans, *Op. cit.*

are a bit more helpful in giving us at least a glimpse of the probable origins of the family before their arrival in Gourdon.

On inspection of the records of the local area – that is to say Kincardineshire and the northern edge of Angus – three Gowan families emerge in the seventeenth century. The first was the Episcopalian family of Dunnottar Parish.[97] There is mention of one of them in the 1640s in Stonehaven,[98] and a few others throughout the century, but they were never particularly numerous. As time wore on into the eighteenth century, they became fairly successful shipmasters and traders, like the Gourdon family (the second of the three families).[99]

The third and oldest known family was the Montrose family. (However, let us always bear in mind that this may simply be the result of the fact that the Montrose records go much further back that the Bervie records.) The first of them was mentioned in 1591.[100] He was Alexander Goway in Ferryden, (perhaps a shipmaster) and represented the town (with others) in a dispute with an English Captain before the Privy Council itself in Edinburgh. What had happened was that the Captain's goods had been seized by a pirate, and then sold on to the Montrosians, and now the Captain was trying desperately to get his goods back. Although ultimately the Montrosians lost the battle, it is at the Montrose marketplace in 1591 that the first man bearing the name Gowan in the area steps on to the pages of history.

After this point, there is a gap in the records, where none of the Montrose Gowans appear, but once again in 1627, shortly after the commencement of the Montrose OPRs, the christening of one Issobell Gowans is recorded, daughter of Robert Gowans, fisher in Montrose. He had three other recorded children – Caterin (c.1628), Robert, (c. 1632) and William, (c. 1635).[101] Note that all of these names are names present in the Gowan family of Gourdon; Robert, Isobel and William appear with great frequency.[102] Robert Gowans himself was mentioned in the Montrose Town Council Minutes on 15th July 1636:-

"Rot Gowans Rot Mylne Jon Skirling Jon Garmack Patrick Ross James Mylne Rot Mackie David Newton for himselff and the maisterie of the bottis quhairof he is awner with their awin consentis actit that they sall not sell any fische fra the tyme they once enter within the water quhill they cum to the fischershoir of this burght And that they sall not pack peill not salt ony fische And sall not suffer any cadger nor uther person to cum within their bottis under the pain of six pundis toties quoties And the haill fisches that they pack peill or salt to be confiscatt"[103]

It would seem, then, that at this stage, the Gowans were shipmasters **but not** owners of the boats they fished from. As shown above, Robert worked for David Newton, who was soon afterwards murdered by another local fisherman who seems to have resented his influence – he was quite a powerful local fish-curer.[104]

---

[97] *Episcopalian Register of the Church of St James the Great* (available at Aberdeen Central Library); Dunnottar OPRs NAS Ref. RD 255

[98] NAS Ref. RS7/5/5

[99] *Episcopalian Records of the Church of St James the Great*

[100] D. Fraser, *Montrose* (1967) at 105. I am grateful to Robert Gove for the suggestion that I should look in the Montrose area for early members of the Gowan family.

[101] Montrose OPRs NAS Ref. RD 312

[102] Bervie OPRs NAS Ref. RD 254

[103] Montrose Town Council Minutes, as cited above, p. 143

[104] See D. G. Adams et al, *The Port of Montrose: A History of its Harbour, Trade and Shipping* (1993)

Apart from this uncertain background of being at the mercy of the owner of the boat, the Gowans in Montrose, along with the other fishermen there, also had to contend with the Magistrates of the Burgh. Intent on ensuring that the people of the town got the best of the catch, they imposed regulation after regulation on the fishers regarding to whom they could sell their fish and under what circumstances they could do this in the 1620s and the 1630s, frequently calling the skippers into the Montrose Tolbooth to enforce the issue.[105] At the very least this must have been annoying to many of the fishermen of the town.

A contemporary of this Robert Gowans was, of course, Jon Gowans in Gourdon, who also eventually became a skipper.[106] The two of them were probably born about the same time, in the early 1600s, judging by the dates of birth of their children.

Can any arguments be formulated that infer a connection of some sort between the Gourdon Gowans and the Montrose Gowans? The first key question to ask pertains to whether or not Jon Gowans was indeed the first of the Gourdon Gowans. I think that he was, but such an argument is difficult. He is certainly the first of the Gourdon Gowans in the Old Parish Records, but he is mentioned in 1644, and the records begin in 1642. One might argue that all this means is that there is no arrival in the village in this period at all; all there is is Jon Gowans, a member of a family who had been in Gourdon for perhaps many years, perhaps very few years – but we cannot with any certainty speak of him as the progenitor, or the first of the family to arrive in the area. Against this, one can set the evidence that there were no other Gowans in Gourdon in this early period; the first of them appears in the mid-1650s, and they could easily have been sons and daughters of the earlier Jon (i.e. born in the mid 1630s and marrying in the mid 1650s). The problem with this argument is that the records are wholly incomplete, and so it is difficult to be certain that the Gowans in the records were indeed the only Gowans in the village at this time. Nonetheless, there is one important point to note – we do have very early Poor Rolls for Bervie Parish in the 1640s – and no Gowans are present on these. There is, for now, no evidence to suggest that Jon Gowans was one of a large family in the village. While the records are not complete enough to allow us to say that absence of evidence is evidence of absence, they are sufficiently complete to allow us to infer from the lack of Gowans in the village in the 1630s that they were not long arrived there. Such an argument could, perhaps, still be attacked due to the fact that large numbers of male members of a family could have been wiped out in a storm in the 1630s, leaving only Jon as a male representative of the line. This effectively happened in the 1730s after the Storm of Wind. Yet if we were dealing with an established family of Gowans one would expect, on the storm theory, some Gowan wives to have been left behind with Gowan children on the Poor Rolls, or sisters, or aunts, or whatever. For this reason, coupled with the OPR evidence, I am willing to put forward the theory that Jon Gowans was indeed the first of the Gourdon Gowans, or at least was a representative of the family during its first or second generation in the village. If this is so, Jon Gowans either was the man, or was in close descent from the man, who came from "ower the hill."[107] If this is the case, then, as stated above, this would in all likelihood place him as coming from the south – the Montrose direction. As has been shown, there was a family of Gowans in Montrose. Oral tradition coupled with the evidence and assumption taken therefrom raises the possibility of a Montrose connection.

---

[105] Montrose Town Council Minutes, as cited above, p. 143
[106] Bervie OPRs NAS Ref. RD 254
[107] Tradition recalled by Mrs Annie Gowans Pittock or Mowat

Secondly, the two families have the same naming patterns – every single name that appears in the Montrose family appears in the early Gourdon family, and vice versa.[108] (Naturally this is by no means conclusive – the names were all reasonably popular at the time – but the point is worth noting.) Thirdly, at this time both families pronounced the "s" on the end of their names – the earliest records in both Bervie and Montrose substantiate this, with the "s" being added to the birth entries for Margaret Gowanes (c. 1642) and Jon Gowans (c. 1646). Also on an altogether less firm argument regarding pronunciation, there may have been an emphasis on the second syllable of the name as Gow**anes** – pronouncing the "anes" part as the "ains" in "rains." This spelling, probably put down phonetically by the Session Clerk, appears in both the Bervie and the Montrose families at different times, and in the case of Alexander Gow**ay** in the 1591 Privy Council Case. The "s" in the Gourdon family seems to have been dropped at a very early date; it last appears in 1646, and only reappears in the mid-nineteenth century as a result of an Anglicisation.[109] Fifthly, the families in Montrose and Gourdon have a great deal in common – they were fisherfolk,[110] but were not particularly well off. Robert Gowans in Montrose was only a skipper, not an owner of a boat.[111] Similarly, with Jon Gowans, he clearly did not start out as the owner of a boat; whether he inherited ownership of Spence's boat later is not clear,[112] but not particularly relevant when trying to establish his status on arrival in Gourdon. Sixthly, Jon Gowans would have had good reason to go to Gourdon. He, by this theory, would have been a junior member of a poor fishing family in a burgh where fishermen were not treated particularly well, and where what freedom they had was constantly in check at the hands of the merchant class. In Gourdon, however, there was only the Laird to please, who was interested in encouraging fishing from his port, not discouraging it.[113] There was also the opportunity eventually to become master of his own boat, rather than forever remaining as a worker on the boat of another. Seventhly, it has to again be stressed that there is no evidence whatsoever to suggest that the Gowans came from either of the neighbouring parishes of Benholm (where there is evidence from the early 1600s that they were not there) or of Kinneff and Catterline (where the OPRs go back to 1616).[114] Therefore, there is compelling evidence to show that the Gowans of Gourdon came from Montrose. As stated, it is possible that Jon and Robert Gowans were brothers, and that they had some connection further back with Alexander Goway of the 1591 case. The Dunnottar family may well have also been a branch of the Montrose family; I am reluctant to say that it was the other way round, due to the oral tradition relating to the "over the hill" issue, and the fact that other names, such as Patrick and James,[115] were preferred by the Dunnottar family to the traditional Montrose and Gourdon names. As well as this, in the 1650s, when reference is found to the Dunnottar family, the name is Gowan, not Gowans.[116] Furthermore, these early Dunnottar Gowans were farm folk, not fisher folk.[117] As such, I do not think that the Dunnottar family is the progenitor family of the Gourdon and Montrose families.

---

[108] Bervie OPRs NAS Ref. RD 254; Montrose OPRs NAS Ref. RD 312
[109] Bervie OPRs; Tradition recalled by Duncan Craig Christie (1904 – 1972)
[110] Bervie OPRs NAS Ref. RD 254; Montrose OPRs NAS Ref. RD 312
[111] Montrose Town Council Minutes, as cited above, p. 152
[112] Bervie OPRs NAS Ref. RD 254
[113] As inferred from the evidence presented in Chapter One
[114] Kinneff and Catterline OPRs NAS Ref. RD 262; NAS Ref. RH15/37/92
[115] *Third Spalding Club Miscellany,* Volume Two, Chamberlain's Account, Dunnottar, 1650-1651
[116] *Ibid*
[117] *Ibid*

That said, this family is quite possibly another off-shoot of the Montrose family, and the pronunciation of the name as "Gowans," as at Gourdon, did not survive contact with the Mearns for long. An outstanding question about this must be as to why Alexander Goway did not pronounce his name with an "s". The only response that I can offer to this is that he did, but that the Clerk at Edinburgh, not knowing him at all well, had written the name quickly and wrongly.

Therefore, it is proposed that the Gowans of Gourdon perhaps came from Montrose before they arrived in Gourdon, probably in the late 1620s or very early 1630s. In the generation after Jon Gowans, three male Gowans appear – Alexander (who married Marjory Mearns in 1671), Robert (who married Katherine Allan in 1665) and John (who married Christian Traill in 1663). There is no evidence that John had any family, but there is proof that Robert and Alexander did.

It is a shame that there is not even a bit more evidence to work with to give greater weight to some of these conclusions about the origins of the Gowans. But the questions make it all the more intriguing, and whatever their roots, once in Gourdon their history was remarkably colourful, filled with the stuff of a great novel. Their many adventures are looked at throughout the rest of this book, in a chronicle of a family of people who were clearly and deeply affected by the times in which they lived.

Part Three: Later Incomers

After this time, and before 1800, many families arrived in Gourdon, each of which played significant roles in the history of the village. By and large, most of their history is covered in the chapters following – mention is made of the early Goves, the Mowats and the Lownies, and the Criggies from Johnshaven, who arrived in the 1730s. Other families too, like the Alexanders, the Collies, the Moirs, the Milnes and the Pirries,[118] played roles in the history of the village, but sadly little has been uncovered in this research about their involvement. Many more arrived in the latter stages of the eighteenth century, as with the Lownies, or in the early years of the nineteenth century, and so, ultimately, there is not a vast amount to say about them within the remit of this history, as one stretching from 1500 to 1800. There were other major families yet to arrive in the village, such as the Craigs from Portlethen,[119] the Coulls from Craig Parish[120] and the Christies from Garvock Parish,[121] but their history lies in the domain of the nineteenth century. So, while little is said of these families here, it most certainly does not diminish the fact that they had a real impact on the history of the village. More attention has been given to the Gowans, the Jeamies and the Ritchies simply because more evidence survives about them and because they, as families, are so bound up with the history of the village that to understand their origins is vital. The purpose of this work, as always, is not to give a wholly complete picture of all of the people of the village during this time – such a task would be difficult, if not impossible – but to draw, from the examples taken from history, a picture of the changing nature of the community.

The true point of this chapter is to provide some basis for understanding the historical background of many individuals in the village, as the point of the last chapter was to provide some basis for the history of the village itself. The history

---

[118] R. Gowans, *Op. cit.*

[119] 1881 Census, Bervie Parish (village of Gourdon)

[120] *Ibid*

[121] 1861 Census, Bervie Parish (village of Gourdon)

shall now turn to look at the changing nature of the relationship between the people and their work, their faith and the law of the land. As shall be demonstrated, it was a dynamic and fascinating relationship showing their true character and giving a much greater insight into the people than the history of the buildings in which they lived, or their own family history in the distant mists of time.

CHAPTER THREE:
FISHING, TRADE AND THE SEA

"...there are eight sloops, or small barks, in all about 300 tons burden,
belonging to Gourdon... It is only in summer that such small vessels... navigate
the seas; in Winter... the sailors betake themselves to fishing, at
least the most industrious of them do so."[122]

Thus Walter Thom described what must be seen as one of the most crucial aspects of the history of the village of Gourdon – its ties with the sea. Of course it was a troubled relationship but one on which the records shed a great deal of light. While the Gourdon men were almost invariably referred to as "fishers" or "sailors" in the Old Parish Registers, as Thom's statement attests,[123] they also did a great deal of trading, travelling and of course smuggling! Towards the end of the eighteenth century, it would seem that it was in the latter occupations that the people of Gourdon made what money they did, until the herring fishing began to pick up in the closing years of the 1790s.

In order to describe both of these livelihoods fully, it is necessary to examine them in two separate sections – one on fishing, one on trade and smuggling. Only then can the full impact of the sea on the community of Gourdon be understood, along with the very real impact that both lines of work had on the character of the people. This would not be complete without reference to the many benefits and extreme dangers experienced by those who lived on what Roy Souter has called *"a wild and rocky coast."*[124]

Section One: Fishing from Gourdon

Fishing was, of course, the main occupation for the people of Gourdon throughout most of the period between 1500 and 1800. There is a reasonable amount of information regarding the occupation that has survived, in particular towards the end of the period being examined. From this a fascinating picture emerges that shows both the dangers and the opportunities that fishing created for the people of the village.

There is a strong possibility that fishing has been carried on at Gourdon from the earliest times. Robert Gowans suggested that the community that used the Werewolf Cairn had used the shore at Gourdon as their harbour.[125] This places the earliest fishing in the area in prehistoric times. More concrete evidence, however, exists to show that there has been a fishing community in the village since 1315, when the "fishertoon of Gurden" was mentioned, in the form of a charter.[126]

---

[122] W. Thom, *Parish of Inverbervie or Bervie*, in Sir John Sinclair (ed.) *Old Statistical Account of Scotland*, Volume XIV – Kincardineshire and South and West Aberdeenshire (1982 reprint) 136-147 at 141-142

[123] W. Thom, *Op. cit.* at 142

[124] R. Souter, *A Wild and Rocky Coast*

[125] R. Gowans, *The Gowans* (1940s) in R. Souter (ed.) *Gourdon and the Surrounding Area – A Compilation of Information and Essays on Local History (unpublished)*

[126] R. Gove, *Gourdon in the Nineteenth Century*, (1980s) (An historical pamphlet published locally based on a talk given by Mr. Gove.)

Much of the earliest material relating to the village concerns trade from Gourdon (see Section Two), but there are fragments of information here and there that refer to every day life for the fishermen and their families in the records before 1700. As discussed in Chapter One and as shall be shown in Section Two of this Chapter, it would appear that Rait of Hallgreen was very keen on encouraging trade from the village of Gourdon, and fishing as well would have been on his agenda of improvement. Hence the move to New Gourdon – away from the old harbour which was *"useless and unfitt for the statione of boattes."*[127] So, as well as trade, fishing can be seen as a pillar of the village economy.

One interesting question at this point would be to ask whose were the boats being fished from, and what types of boats were being used, at this early period. Some fairly large craft were possibly being used at neighbouring Johnshaven. A document from this period (see Appendix Three)[128] shows seven groupings of sailors in the village, arranged in groupings of six to eight. These may have been the seven crews of seven boats in Johnshaven at the time. If this were the case, it would appear that the typical crew of a large fishing vessel on the Kincardineshire coast would have been between six and eight fishermen. As shown earlier, several early names appear in the records of Gourdon fishers and shipmasters – Andrew Mearns and David Todd (fishers in 1618)[129] and Jon Spence, Jon Gowans[130] and Robert Andersone[131] (shipmasters in Gourdon in the 1630s and 1640s). All of these men were probably both traders and fishermen. What trade there was was probably carried on in the summer months, when it would have been easier for the small trading sloops worked by the villagers.[132] The fishing would have been carried out throughout the year, but it would have dominated work in the winter.

Luckily, at this early period, there is reference in the neighbouring village of Crawton to the varieties of fish caught by the men of Gourdon. There were four skippers there and they caught mainly skate, keillings and small fish. Of these, their collective rent to the Earl Marischall was, between 1st January 1650 and 21st October 1650:

"of sket 38 at 5/- the piece [sic], of Keilling [large cod] 39 at 4/- ye peice, ane turbitt 13/4, of small fish 1400 at 10/- per hunder is £24/14/4"[133]

Of the catch itself, as shown above, much went on rent to the Laird, but some would have been kept back for food. Anything remaining would have been left largely to the women of the village to sell off as best they could. Often this meant walking for miles to markets like the one at Montrose to get the best prices for their fish. This task of the womenfolk never changed throughout the seventeenth or eighteenth centuries.

Although little is directly recorded in this period about the work of the women in the village with regard to the fishing, they clearly played a very great role in ensuring that the voyage was successful. Even though there is evidence that the men

---

[127] NAS Ref. RH15/37/133

[128] NAS Ref. RH15/37/192

[129] R. Gove, *Op. cit.*

[130] Inverbervie OPRs

[131] L. B. Taylor (ed.) *Aberdeen Shorework Accounts 1596-1670* (1972) at 215

[132] W. Thom, *Parish of Inverbervie or Bervie*, in Sir John Sinclair (ed.) *Old Statistical Account of Scotland*, Volume XIV – Kincardineshire and South and West Aberdeenshire (1982 reprint) 136-147 at 141-142

[133] Third Spalding Club, *Miscellany II*, (1940) at 200

folk took a role in baiting the lines at this time, (David Fatt was convicted of doing so in 1676 on the Sabbath)[134] in later times it was very much part of the work of the womenfolk to do this. Besides this they would have to sell the fish and look after their families, which were often very extensive and ensure that any other food that had to be bought to supplement the family diet was bought (as seen in the case, in 1778,[135] when it was the women of Gourdon who challenged Robert Napier, the Bervie merchant, to hand over meal in a time of hunger, not the men – see Chapter Five). The women also seem often to have been very much involved in either supporting (or even instigating) attempts to "right wrongs" in the area, as in 1778. So their role in the seventeenth century, in particular with regard to the fishing, was just as important as that of the men of the village, but sadly not as well documented. However, they were always sure to stay away from the pier when the men were heading out to sea – such a presence was said to be bad luck by the Gourdon men.[136]

As for the type of lines used, there is less evidence relating directly to Gourdon at this period. However, information does exist as to the types of boats used by the fishermen at this time. Apart from the sloops, which were probably primarily for trading, on April 29th 1658, it was noted in the Aberdeen Shore Work Accounts that three shillings had been received for *"anckraidge from ane small yoll from Gurdon."*[137] This is perhaps a reference to one of the Gourdon fishing "fleet," and tells something of the type of fishing being carried on there at the time. These boats, judging from later sources, had small crews, one Gourdon "yaul" having only three men aboard in 1792.[138] The design for the boats seems to have spread from the north, and may have its roots in Norse boat-building.[139] According to James Miller, in "Salt in the Blood," the Fair Isle yole was between twenty and twenty-two feet in length, with a fifteen foot keel, a beam of five and a half feet and a draught of three feet.[140] It would seem, then, that much of the fishing at this date was small-scale and largely inshore. At Gourdon, as had probably been the case for centuries, the fishermen used the famous "half-mile stene" to tell when they were half way between Bervie and Gourdon. To this day the stone still stands out markedly from the rocks on the beach between the two communities.

There is no record of any larger boats in Gourdon itself before 1730, but it would seem very likely that there had been some larger craft, judging by the efforts of Rait of Hallgreen to otherwise improve the village and judging by the fact that there may have been some larger boats in Johnshaven at the time. So, in the Gourdon harbour, in the last years of the seventeenth century, there were probably a few yauls, some sloops and perhaps two or three larger fishing boats.

Because of the fact that some boats were often fairly small, added risk came with them. Apart from the dreadful storm of 1588, which claimed one of the mighty Spanish Galleons, there was another *"tempest"* on February 29th 1648 that caused the fishers great "distress," and this was acted upon by the Kirk Session.[141] This shows

---

[134] NAS Ref. CH2/34/11
[135] J. Andersen, *Black Book of Kincardineshire* (1879) at 81-83
[136] Tradition recalled by Elinor Marjorie Christie
[137] L. Taylor, *Op. cit.* at 416
[138] W. Thom, *Parish of Inverbervie or Bervie*, in Sir John Sinclair (ed.) *Old Statistical Account of Scotland*, Volume XIV – Kincardineshire and South and West Aberdeenshire (1982 reprint) 136-147 at 142
[139] J. Miller, *Salt in the Blood* (1999) at 25-26
[140] *Ibid*
[141] NAS Ref. CH2/34/10

how precarious was the situation of the fishermen. Circumstances like these probably helped to encourage the strong tradition of superstition among the villagers.

Essentially this concludes the background information to the more extensive history of fishing in Gourdon in the eighteenth century. By the late seventeenth century, the village harbour had been moved to a more suitable location (see Chapter One), more men were coming to the village, seeking work as fishermen, and there were quite a few boats, hoping to take advantage of the good days for the fishing to come.

As the eighteenth century dawned, the fishing was set to become more prosperous for a few years. Unfortunately, this did not save the Rait family of Hallgreen, the last of the Raits having ended up bankrupt and ruined in the 1720s.[142]

But by the same period, families like the Gowans were beginning to be more successful. One story in particular infers that one of the Gowans may have owned three sloops at one time.[143] While some degree of this prosperity must have been down to trade, a substantial amount of it would have been down to the more successful fishing of the day. At this time, haddocks were mainly caught by the Gourdon fishers, and this type of fish continued to be the main source of income throughout the first eighty years of the eighteenth century.[144]

The signs of an increasing income in this period are very evident. For example, Jock Gowan, who lived in the early eighteenth century, was illiterate,[145] but his own grandson, John Gowan, (b. 1756), son of Robert Gowan, was able to write.[146] An education did not come cheap at the school at Bervie, so clearly Robert Gowan had more disposable income than his father had had. Perhaps more directly relevant to the fishing, it would seem that the Gourdon shipmasters viewed investing in their vessels as worthwhile, which indicates that fishing was becoming a more successful occupation. This fact is illustrated in a rental of Hallgreen Estate dating from 1769,[147] which shows that of all the many boats in the harbour at Gourdon, only one was owned by the Laird of Hallgreen. Since the Laird of Arbuthnott at the same time does not seem to have owned any of the Gourdon boats,[148] this would suggest that many of the Gourdon shipmasters were also ship-owners. (Naturally greater certainty on this point would be established following a perousal of the rentals of other lairds in the area, but the Arbuthnotts and the lairds of Hallgreen seem to have been the main landowners in the area.) Again, this shows that the source of the income, the fishing, was profitable, and that the fishermen viewed continued investment in the industry as wise. It also shows a growing ability on the part of the villagers to control their own fate.

But the sea was still remarkably dangerous. On February 20th 1730, almost exactly eighty-two years after the last major disaster for the people of Gourdon at sea, a terrible storm struck, called by the then Session-Clerk the "Storm of Wind." It was recorded in the Old Parish Registers thus:

---

[142] Information researched by Robert Gove

[143] R. Gowans, *Op. cit.*

[144] W. Thom, *Parish of Inverbervie or Bervie*, in Sir John Sinclair (ed.) *Old Statistical Account of Scotland*, Volume XIV – Kincardineshire and South and West Aberdeenshire (1982 reprint) 136-147 at 142-143

[145] Bervie OPRs NAS Ref. RD 254

[146] NAS Ref. SC5/8/116 (Process dated 1786-1787 involving Robert Gowan, Ann Criggie and their eldest son John Gowan (b. 1756)

[147] NAS Ref. SC5/76/29

[148] Arbuthnott family papers (University of Aberdeen Archives) (Various rentals in the period in question were examined on this point.)

"This Alexander Freeman, with over eight persons fishers in Gourdon were lost at sea in a dreadful hurricane on the 20th of February last, the names of them were Simon Gibson, David Fatt, Alexander Gowan, William Gowan, David Jeammie, Alexander Jeammie, Robert Welsh, William Gowan and the said Alexander Freeman."[149]

As stated by Robert Gowans, it would appear that this record was inserted in the OPRs as Alexander Freeman's child was baptised after his death. One can imagine what the loss of eight working men would have meant to a fishing community like Gourdon, and to their families. The Kirk did what it could, and supported the poor families left behind as much as was possible, in some cases for the next twenty-four years.[150] According to Gowans, the disaster left one hundred and fourteen widows and fatherless children between Mathers and Cowie.[151]

But Gourdon did recover, albeit very much scarred. By the 1760s, the fishing reached its height in the eighteenth century, as described by Walter Thom.[152] At this time there were three large fishing boats in the village, along with several smaller vessels and, of course, the sloops themselves, which gave employment to thirty fishermen.[153] And, of course, it was by this time that the ownership of the vessels had transferred to the fishermen themselves. This growing prosperity may have been one of the factors that attracted James Mowat from Kinneff to set up his weaving business in Gourdon in the 1760s.[154]

Sadly, this height of success did not last for long. In the early 1770s, several fishermen were brought before the Sheriff Court at Stonehaven,[155] being sued to pay back debts, showing that, for many in the village, the more prosperous times were coming to an end. Food shortages in the late 1770s came to a head in 1778 with the Meal Mob Riots (see Chapter Five), further showing that, in such times, the fishing was already no longer adequate to support the needs of the families. The fatal blow to the Gourdon fishing industry of the eighteenth century came in 1782. Thom described, in this year, a *"prodigious storm... on this coast, the wind blowing with uncommon violence, ... [raising]... the sea with mountainous billows, as to produce effects almost like an earthquake."*[156] After this disaster, the haddock fishing, possibly already in difficulties, judging from the troubles of the 1770s, failed almost completely. Thom was of the view that this was due to the fact that the storm had destroyed the mussels on the bed of the sea that the haddocks fed on, and so this situation, as Thom said, *"behoved the haddocks to move to a more favourable station."* Whatever, the Gourdon fishing industry was in trouble in this period.

---

[149] Bervie OPRs NAS Ref. RD 254

[150] NAS Ref. CH2/34/6

[151] R. Gowans, *Op. cit.*

[152] W. Thom, *Parish of Inverbervie or Bervie*, in Sir John Sinclair (ed.) *Old Statistical Account of Scotland*, Volume XIV – Kincardineshire and South and West Aberdeenshire (1982 reprint) 136-147 at 142-143

[153] *Ibid* at 142

[154] Bervie OPRs NAS Ref. RD 254; tradition recalled by Mrs Annie Pittock (nee Mowat) (1909-2004); tradition recalled by Jessie Smith Christie (nee Moncur) (1904-1982)

[155] NAS Ref. SC5/8/92; M/P/15/148/7; NAS Ref. SC5/8/93; cf NAS Ref. SC5/8/115-116

[156] W. Thom, *Parish of Inverbervie or Bervie*, in Sir John Sinclair (ed.) *Old Statistical Account of Scotland*, Volume XIV – Kincardineshire and South and West Aberdeenshire (1982 reprint) 136-147 at 143

This saw the end of Gourdon as a strong fishing port in this period – it would be another thirty to forty years before the fishing would recover. During this time, only the older members of the fishing community continued to fish from the village – by 1792 there were only twelve *"old and decrepid"* men so employed, who earned *"but a scanty pittance."*[157] It would seem that these earnings were largely based on the income from the cod fisheries, cod costing five or six times as much as it had previously done. However, the village itself did survive the period, due to the fact that trade and smuggling boomed.[158] The younger men in the village were thus employed, and their families would eventually become fishers in Gourdon once again. Even in 1792, Walter Thom could see the light at the end of the tunnel. He spoke of the "good number of herring" that had been taken in the years before he wrote of his account, the herring priced at three pence per dozen.[159] Shortly Gourdon, along with the rest of the East Coast of Scotland, would be drawn into the hunt for the silver darlings.

The connection of the Gourdon folk with the sea perhaps had a deeper significance. Life was indeed hard for eighteenth century fishing communities like Gourdon. It involved an ongoing struggle with the sea and the elements, yet since these communities looked to the sea, and not to the land, for their living, they perhaps enjoyed an independence of mind that would have been absent in the lives of their landward counterparts – the subtenants and cottars at this time. As my grandfather once remarked, *"the fisher folk were freer than the land folk."*[160]

Arguably, the destinies of those who worked as fishermen and traders in a village like Gourdon were not governed to the same extent by the decisions of lairds or wealthier tenant farmers. It would, of course, be unwise to generalise about this status of "freedom" in this period; for example, the fishermen in Auchmithie, bonded serfs as they were until the late eighteenth century, would not have felt any freer than the land folk. But Gourdon was not Auchmithie. Furthermore, in the Gourdon area, the lairds were improvers, and there the people often seem to have owned their own vessels, and to have had greater control over their lives than their counterparts in fishing villages elsewhere in Scotland. At any rate, in the next few chapters, it will be shown that the people of Gourdon in their dealings with the kirk and the courts of law did indeed have something of an independent nature, often refusing to obey blindly the authority of these institutions. Perhaps the greater freedom from the lairds that the people of Gourdon enjoyed (which, if one is to give any credit here to the improving mentality, was in part down to the enlightened attitudes of the lairds themselves) engendered in them a confidence to defend themselves against the excesses of those in authority.

---

[157] *Ibid*

[158] CE53/1/6-14

[159] W. Thom, *Parish of Inverbervie or Bervie*, in Sir John Sinclair (ed.) *Old Statistical Account of Scotland*, Volume XIV – Kincardineshire and South and West Aberdeenshire (1982 reprint) 136-147 at 143

[160] Tradition recalled by Duncan Craig Christie (1904-1972)

From the earliest times it is possible that some sort of trade was carried out from the old port of Gourdon. As mentioned above, in 1315,[161] there was reference to the original "ferm and fishertoon" of Gourdon, and doubtless this was the original seaport bearing the name, situated at Mudlin's Den. However, it would seem unlikely that there was much trade from the village at this early stage, due to the lack of a substantial harbour there. As stated by Robert Gove, the fishers at this time were possibly bonded serfs of the Laird of Hallgreen.

But by 1506, all of this had begun to change. Trade was underway from Gourdon, and it is likely that by this date the village of New Gourdon had been founded to allow this to be possible (see Chapter One). At this time, wool, hides and salt fish were exported from the village[162] – but not salmon. The merchants of Montrose had ensured that it was only through that Royal Burgh that this commodity could be exported in the area. If it is correct that the village of New Gourdon was underway by 1506, it shows that the Lairds had an improving mentality at an astoundingly early date.

There is further evidence to show that the Lairds were keenly involved in developing the village as a trading base, and that they were aware of how this could be used to their advantage. In 1549, David Rait of Drumnagair and Hallgreen possibly built the first known Shore Inn at "Gerdoun." As stated earlier, it was at this time simply known as the "Girnel House." It is likely that this was at New Gourdon, where the passing traders would stop, and it was constructed at the *"hawyning place"* of the village. This mysterious place might have been the same area in the village today that slopes down William Street by the Monument towards the harbour, where, in ancient times, the boats might have been hauled up on to the shore (hence the name – "hauling" and "winding" mixed together). This first inn may even have been on the same site as the later one dating from 1650 (see Chapter One). Clearly David Rait thought that the inn would be a success, as he leased it to someone whom he would have wanted to do well – his son, John Rait, the earliest inhabitant of the village whose name has survived.[163]

Over the next hundred and fifty years, Gourdon was fought over by the Lairds of Hallgreen and the Viscounts of Arbuthnott.[164] Perhaps this indicates that the trading was becoming quite lucrative, further shown by the increasing number of Victual Houses in the village by 1599. By 1601, James VI had even given the people of the village the right to trade in food on the moors and marshes of Bervie.[165] Exports were also increasing, and from 1638 to 1639 five ships arrived in Leith from Gourdon on trading business, compared to four from Stonehaven and three from St Andrews.[166] Although these earliest traders had all originated from other ports before coming to the village, it does show that Gourdon was fast becoming a fairly important trading centre on the coast of the Mearns, rivalling Stonehaven and the rapidly growing new economic adversary, Johnshaven. The growing opportunities in Gourdon may have attracted one man to the village – Jon Gowans, who probably

---

[161] R. Gove, *Gourdon's Story*, (1980s) A pamphlet published locally
[162] *Ibid*
[163] NAS Ref. RH15/37/8
[164] NAS Ref. RH15/37/118
[165] R. Gove, *Gourdon's Story*, (1980s)
[166] McNeill and H. MacQueen, *Atlas of Scottish History to 1707*, (1996) at 272

arrived in the 1630s, and was perhaps the founder of one of the largest families in the village (see Chapter Two).

However, records of trade during this early period are scarce. The Shore Inn, the only place in the village that might have been a focus for imported goods, is not well documented. There is reference to David Law in Gourdon selling alcohol on October 29th 1676,[167] which may imply that at that date he was Tacksman of the Shore Inn and that someone was importing alcohol through the harbour at Gourdon for him to sell. But aside from this there is little to go on to draw conclusions about the amount of trade in seventeenth century Gourdon. What would seem certain is that the Lairds of Hallgreen were keen to encourage it, this probably being one of their reasons for moving the village south in the early 1500s. By 1694, a writ relating to Gourdon in their papers seems to attest that the move was complete. The impulse for trade and bigger fishing boats had caused Old Gourdon to cease to exist.

It is perhaps an historical irony that it was only with the introduction of the hated Customs Taxes imposed by Westminster that we can begin to gain a greater insight into the lives of the people of Gourdon and how trade affected them. The village came under the administration of Montrose Outport, but some time passed before the Collector started trying to impose the restrictions on trade he had to in Gourdon.

It was by the 1760s that the trade, and subsequent smuggling, in Gourdon had caused enough concern for a Tidesman to be appointed to oversee the collection of customs at the village on behalf of the Collector.[168] What this does clearly show is that trade must have been developing to a great extent in the early eighteenth century, at both Gourdon and Johnshaven, and this is certainly supported by the oral traditions surrounding the village at the time.

According to Andrew Lownie, a nineteenth century descendant of the Gowan family, the buying and selling of goods did play quite a role in the history of the family.[169] Cross-referencing his story with recently unearthed material, the tale may perhaps be placed into the context of a timeline. However, before considering how to identify the various (un-named) people in the story, it is perhaps useful to lay out the stories in their original forms.

One of the fishers of Gourdon (perhaps a grandson or a great-grandson of the man I believe to have been the original Gowan in Gourdon, Jon Gowans) had three sloops, from which he had probably previously carried out his trading ventures. When he died his widow gave the three sloops to their three sons. One of the sons was "our" ancestor – Andrew Lownie used the term to refer to the ancestor who was common to him and to Robert Gowans. He is supposed to have been the keeper of the Shore Inn in the early eighteenth century.[170] According to the story the brothers "made trips to Holland for grog to the Shore Inn."[171] In short, they were establishing a small family business, cutting out the need for a middleman to provide their alcohol for the Inn. It is also said that at this time they often went to Dysart (a great Fife

---

[167] NAS Ref. CH2/34/11

[168] F. Wilkins, *The Smuggling Story of the Northern Shores* (1995) Chapter 9

[169] R. Gowans, *Op. cit.*

[170] The actual tradition was that Alexander Gowan, husband of Helen Kemlo, was the grandson of the Shore Inn folk, and it appears that the tradition referred to his paternal grandfather – time and again I have been told by various family members that it was the *Gowans* who had the Shore Inn – not the Criggie who was Alexander's maternal grandfather.

[171] R. Gowans, *Op. cit.*

"emporium" of goods, especially from the Netherlands, as noted by Gowans), sometimes, perhaps, with the purpose of buying necessities for the Shore Inn in mind.

However, the travelling backwards and forwards to the Netherlands had some interesting outcomes! The third of the Gowan brothers (whose name is not certain), took his sloop to Holland one year, but possibly left too late in the summer to return before the seas became too dangerous for his ship. Whether he was thus compelled to do so or not, Gowan did stay there all winter, and seems to have managed to master enough of the local tongue to strike a bargain with a Dutchman. Imagine the shock of his mother, then, when he arrived the following spring, back in Gourdon, minus his sloop but with a Dutch Lugger instead! He had done a swap.[172]

But there was worse. On February 21st 1730, the twenty-four year old James Gowan, (the only person named in the story), was returning home from a trip to Dysart. It was night, and the skipper decided to go down below for a while, his crew, an old man and a boy, being left in charge. Unfortunately he fell asleep, only to be re-awakened shortly afterwards by the sound of a gale outside – the infamous "Storm of Wind," (see Section One of this chapter) – which had driven his sloop on to the rocks, the smashing of the wood and the roar of the sea echoing through every fibre of his being. Hurriedly he leapt out of his cabin and rushed on to the deck, and realised that the sloop was stuck fast on the rocks (this was to the north of Bervie Bay, at Roger's Haven). The storm in full spate, there was nothing he could do, but order his crew to escape while they could. Gowan quickly returned to his cabin, to collect what personal possessions he could. He then rushed back out and slipped over the ship's bows to safety. His mother then made her way along with the Gourdon people to see what could be done. Perhaps Gowan was rather concerned about what his mother would say when she found out that her boat had been wrecked!

When his mother arrived, it was to find her boat indeed wrecked and the old man and the boy fighting over who had been to blame. But her son was long gone, away down the road to the south. The mother in question was not, however, the sort of lady to be stopped in her tracks by this. She returned to Gourdon and, presumably once the grieving for the other victims of the Storm of Wind was over, she prepared to go south to see her son. She was by then in her late sixties, or possibly even her early seventies, but age seems to have been little barrier to her purposes! When James heard his mother was marching south to meet him, he realised that he was beaten, and walked some of the way himself back north to meet up with her. It cannot have been an easy rendezvous.

In spite of this, James Gowan and his mother seem to have sorted out the difference, as he regularly corresponded with her until her death when the family lost trace of him. The last anyone knew of him was that he was the master of a three masted schooner sailing from Leith (no small achievement for someone who had begun his career by sinking a sloop). The older people of Gourdon said that the Gowans in St Monance were descended from him.[173]

Who were these people? Perhaps more pertinent is the question "when were these people alive?" Gowans himself tried to answer the question, basing his conclusions on a dating of the story given to him by an elderly family member, which placed the incident in the first half of the eighteenth century. He himself admitted *"I really do not know where to place these men in the records."* However, the conclusions he tried to draw from the evidence he had seem sound to me. (This is

---

[172] *Ibid*
[173] *Ibid*

dealt with in more detail in Appendix Five.) First of all, he proposed that the man referred to as "our" ancestor was the earliest ancestor remembered by his father – John, or Jock Gowan. It is easy enough to see why. He identified Jock Gowan with John Gowan who had several children in the 1730s, and it seems almost certain that this John was the ancestor of the later Gowans of Gourdon, including Andrew Lownie and Gowans himself. This being so, the James Gowan who lost his sloop at sea would have been Jock's brother, as would have been the Gowan who swapped his ship for a Dutch lugger.

What about the parents of James, Jock and the anonymous Gowan? I am not entirely sure why, but Gowans did suggest that the father of all three men could have been Alexander Gowan, whose son Alexander was born in 1699. As far as Gowans knew, he was the first recorded Gowan in Gourdon. In his time the parish records for Bervie prior to 1698 appeared to have been lost; they were in fact added to the collection in the NAS in the 1970s, including Kirk Session records and (highly intermittent) OPRs dating from the 1640s. Access to these records renders one aware that there were, in fact, several other male Gowans in the village at the time who could have fathered James and Jock. Furthermore, while the OPRs seem to have been kept quite regularly from 1670, there is a four-year gap between 1695 and 1699. This makes it very difficult to come to any definite conclusion about the parentage of these brothers. The more likely candidates are the three couples who records prove were having children in the 1690s – John Gowan and Margaret Mearns, Alexander Gowan and Christian Milne and Alexander Gowan and Marie Mearns. Matters are not helped by the fact that James Gowan's birth was not recorded (he should have been baptised in 1706 if he was twenty-four at the time of the Storm of Wind). In short, we really cannot be certain who were the parents of Jock and James Gowan. We know that one Alexander Gowan was on poor relief in the late 1720s, and then ceased to be on poor relief in 1729 – perhaps he died. In any event, we could probably eliminate him as a potential candidate for the father of the three brothers – how could a man end up on poor relief when he owned three sloops? (If nothing else perhaps this will help to illustrate for the reader the problems of constructing family trees for this period in time!)

What I think that we *can* say is that there was a single family of Gowans in the village in this period. All of the Gowans always considered themselves related to one another. I think that Robert Gowans in his history of the family was quite correct to identify John Gowan, whose children were born in the 1730s, with Jock Gowan, who must still remain, in spite of all the research done, the earliest known ancestor in the particular line of Gowans from whom Andrew Lownie and Robert Gowans descended. But I think that it is to go too far (and I think that Gowans was merely speculating when he suggested the point in any event) to say with certainty that John's father was the Alexander whose son was born in 1699.

Jock Gowan seems to have led a more settled lifestyle. He kept the Shore Inn, continued in his trading trips, married and had a family,[174] and never got into trouble with the Customs Officers[175] or the Kirk![176] As shown in the next chapter, he was so well thought of that he was even asked to be an elder.[177] He was a most unusual Gowan, but did not set a trend. His sons were to prove as colourful through their successes and their misdemeanours as any of their predecessors. It may actually have

---

[174] Bervie OPRs NAS Ref. RD 254
[175] CE53/1/1-3
[176] NAS Ref. CH2/34/11-15; NAS Ref. CH2/34/1
[177] NAS Ref. CH2/34/14; NAS Ref. CH2/34/1

been the smuggling activities of his eldest son, Robert, (b. 1731)[178] that helped to spur the perceived need for a Tidesman at Gourdon, along with one other very simple need – the need for fuel, and, in particular, coal. (Robert was the only Robert Gowan in the village at this time and is identified as the son of Jock from the line recalled in oral tradition by Gowans.)

In the Statistical Account of 1792,[179] Thom described the history of the changing fuel sources for Gourdon. In the early 1760s, the village required only fifty bolls Scots of coals to satisfy the need for fuel every year, due to the fact that labour was cheap and peat mosses were plentiful nearby, and so it was less expensive to use peat than it was to use coal on the fires.

However, during the next thirty years the demand on coal became greater and greater, until by 1792, the mosses were "nearly exhausted." As a result, over this period, the import of coal into Gourdon grew, until by Thom's day about eight hundred bolls Scots of coals (two thousand barrels English) were passing through Gourdon and on to the countryside "for a few miles around."[180] Whoever could corner the market on coal would be rather successful, as, during this period, it became a vital commodity.

But there was a snag. Walter Thom was entirely correct when he stated that, on coal, there was levied *"a partial and unjust tax... expensive to the manufacturer and oppressive to the poor; a tax, which by no means can yield to Government a compensation adequate to its extensive oppression and pernicious effects."*[181] (Quite out of character for Walter Thom – he probably liked paying for his coal as little as everyone else!) Of course, there was a solution – smuggling! And the records are rich with the trading adventures of the villagers.

The first definite reference to smuggling at Gourdon (although doubtless it had been carried on for generations before) came in 1767. Previously the Gourdon people had, to a large extent, been at liberty to carry on their smuggling free of the notice of the Montrose Collector, in his office at the Castlestead. Perhaps he was quite happy to allow this situation to continue, his real "headache" being the ring of very powerful and successful Montrose smugglers. But on September 2nd 1767, he received a letter that forced him to start investigating the village. It was the beginning of thirty years of trouble!

The letter,[182] which had come from the Customs Officers of Edinburgh, directed the Collector to *"Enquire and Report... from the best information which can be obtained the Circumstances and Character of Robert Gowans of Gourdon."* How Gowan (son of John (Jock) Gowan mentioned above) had managed to attract the attention of the Customs Officers in Edinburgh is unknown. Possibly his smuggling from the Forth Valley area (he later traded with Clackmannan[183] in coal and alcohol and he probably also traded from Dysart[184]) had caught their watchful eye, and they wanted to know whom they were dealing with. The response[185] was brief.

---

[178] Inverbervie OPRs NAS Ref. RD 254

[179] W. Thom, *Parish of Inverbervie or Bervie*, in Sir John Sinclair (ed.) *Old Statistical Account of Scotland,* Volume XIV – Kincardineshire and South and West Aberdeenshire (1982 reprint) 136-147 at 142

[180] *Ibid*

[181] *Ibid*

[182] CE53/2/6

[183] D. Dobson, *Mariners of Aberdeen and Northern Scotland* (Available at Stonehaven Library)

[184] R. Gowans, *Op. cit.*

[185] CE53/1/6

Having *"laid themselves out as much as possible,"* three days after the letter was sent (it seems that they did not *"lay themselves out"* for a very long time) they replied:

> *"we learn he is often employed in smuggling, being*
> *a Skipper of a small fishing boat, and is a drunken fellow,*
> *and as to the last, he is very low and poor."*

Quite a condemnation! This is, of course, a rather interesting piece of evidence – the first direct evidence as to the character of an inhabitant of Gourdon. But is it fair, based on what we know of Gowan? It is true that he was a smuggler. However, in defence of Robert Gowan, one should remember several things. We do not know who the source of the *"best information"* was, but we do know that there were many "well-wishers" in the area (see below) who might have represented people whom they did not like in a very unfavourable light. Secondly, *"low and poor"* as he was, Gowan still managed to put up a gravestone for his daughter, Isobel, when she died in 1784, which is still standing. Only two other Gourdon tombstones have survived from this period,[186] and clearly it was an expensive business to put one up. So Gowan did care for his family, showing some decency to his character. In defence of the collector's account, however, at the time Gowan was described as *"low and poor"* we have no information as to the financial circumstances of the family – they improved as the century wore on. What we do know is that Gowan didn't care for taxes. This was certainly enough to result in his condemnation.

With this investigation (and probably others like it) completed, the Collector had to take action to regain control over the Gourdon smugglers.[187] He hoped as well, perhaps, to restrict in the process the activities of the two most powerful Bervie smugglers – Walter Sime and Robert Napier, who were soon to be joined by one who seems to have been almost a professional smuggler – James Strachan. He spent his early years breaking the law, failed miserably in the process, ending up bankrupt, and then made a shrewd career move by 1772, becoming a Writer and a Messenger for the courts (this was how he styled himself, anyway, and he was to have frequent dealings with the Gourdon people). The move from law-breaker to law-keeper was only skin deep, however; he remained a smuggler at heart.[188] The three of them presided over a smuggling empire, with contracts up and down the coast, Gourdon being a company branch managed by the Jamies and the Gowans! In the end, the Customs Officers would fail to bring Sime and Napier to heel – but where the Collector failed, the Gourdon people succeeded, when they were cheated by Napier and turned on their former employer, in 1778 (see Chapter Five).[189] And no one can claim that the Officers did not try to act. (It should be noted at the outset of this discussion that much work has been done in this area already by Frances Wilkins in her book *The Smuggling of the Northern Shores*; points derived from her work are, of course, acknowledged in the footnotes.)

Wilkins notes that the first of the Gourdon tidesmen, Phillips, was rewarded for his efforts on one occasion by a smuggler by having one of his eyes punched so hard that it came out of its socket. In the end, in accordance with the testimony of James and Alexander Gowan (probably brothers of Robert Gowan who was born in

---

[186] Maxwell et al. (ed) *Pre-1855 Gravestones – Kincardineshire* (1986)
[187] CE53/1/6
[188] F.Wilkins, *Op. cit.* p. 112
[189] J. Andersen, *The Black Book of Kincardineshire* (1879) at 81-83

1731) and one Robert Watt in Gourdon, Phillips was caught in the act of collusion with the smugglers. By 1777, (by which time Gourdon had managed to convert two more tidesmen to smuggling!) Phillips's conduct was described as bearing *"every mark of insanity or intoxication."* His brush with Gourdon seems to have been too much for him![190]

In this period, frequent smuggling, such as that employed by Robert Gowan, went unpunished. To illustrate the point, in July 1773 Gowan had escaped reprimand after smuggling fifty-four casks and cases to Milton of Mathers for James Inverarity, who was a bankrupt cooper in Arbroath.[191] It is interesting again to note that the extent of this smuggling network can be demonstrated here to have covered a large stretch of coastline.

Accordingly, in 1775, a "stout and vigorous young man,"[192] called Thomas Mills replaced Rodger, the previous tidesman. It was hoped he would bring some order back to the collection of dues at Gourdon. However, it was to prove a vain hope. Unlike Phillips, he refused to collude with the smugglers; as a result several of them, led by Andrew Jamie and Alexander Gowan, tried to blacken his character to ensure his dismissal, and to make his stay in the village rather uncomfortable (there is a wonderful reference in the records to a drunken fray in the village during which a jug of ale was thrown at the hapless tidesman – it was Robert Gowan who testified as to this point). They failed in this, but by 1777 it was clear that he had lost control of the smugglers in Gourdon, and so he was posted to Ferryden.

In the place of Mills, two new tidesmen – William Buchanan and John Sharp – were appointed at Gourdon. They were as allied to the smugglers as Rodger had been, but were better at covering their tracks, and they survived almost eight years in the village. Smuggling thrived.[193]

But the Collector, for now, knew nothing of this. Wilkins notes that he was planning to have a boat fitted out for the service of the customs, to monitor the shores in a bid to help tackle the smugglers. One of the members of the crew of this boat was to be Alexander Gowan, who, because of his extensive knowledge of the smuggling up and down the coast, was selected.[194]

However, there was a problem. On 25th June 1777, one who signed himself "A Well Wisher," wrote to the Customs Officers at Edinburgh, that:-

"I can't help acquainting your Honours that
Gowan is a very improper man for said service [working on the customs boat] *when he often aided and assisted the smugglers, even personally, for which it consists with my knowledge he was well rewarded."*[195]

When asked to comment on the situation, the Collector stated that Gowan had previously worked on the boat of a smuggler but had been convicted of no wrongdoing personally. He went on to state that the so-called "well-wisher" was probably one of those people Gowan had reported to the Customs Officers previously for smuggling.

---

[190] F. Wilkins, *Op. cit.* p. 142
[191] *Ibid*
[192] *Ibid* p. 142-146
[193] *Ibid* p. 146-152
[194] *Ibid* p. 173-174
[195] *Ibid* p. 173-174

But, over the next few weeks, questions came up regarding the validity of the evidence Gowan had given to the Court earlier on. Finally, after many such allegations had mounted up, he was forced to resign from the crew of the customs boat on August 12th 1777. Immediately he left on a "voyage to the Firth of Forth," and did not return until September 2nd. He would have to console himself in his loss of earnings with trade.

Like Alexander, Robert Gowan continued to make these trading trips south well into his fifties. His sloop, the *Ann* of Gourdon,[196] probably named after his wife, Ann Criggie, imported coal to Gourdon, while it might, like some of the other sloops in the village, have exported grain.[197] This was the major export at the time, with about four thousand bolls Scots of grain[198] leaving Gourdon per annum, and these were usually carried either to the Firth of Forth or, later on, to Glasgow and Greenock by the Forth-Clyde Canal.[199] Tradition also has it that lime was imported into Gourdon by the Gowans;[200] it certainly did come into the village after 1768, to be used as fertiliser on the nearby farms.[201] So even if fishing was failing in the period after 1782, as shown in section one of this chapter, trade was expanding rapidly.

But the older generation were getting to the stage where it was no longer possible for them to continue to do much of the trading further afield due to their advanced years. By 1786, Robert Gowan was actually fifty-five. He decided that he wanted to pass on the living from the *Ann* to his third son, Alexander, who was then only eighteen. (Again, for these relationships, see Appendix Five.) His elder surviving son, Robert, was already established as a trader, while his youngest, James, was still only sixteen. While Robert Gowan, the father, was to remain the owner of the boat until his death, Alexander, the son, became its Master. He probably continued to use it, as his father had done, to trade in coal from Alloa,[202] as the fishing was by this stage in great decline.

Still, even in this occupation the young Alexander Gowan was not safe. In the 1780s, at some point after he became the Shipmaster of the *Ann*, he had a fearsome quarrel with his father, the owner. In his fury, Robert Gowan stormed out of his home and left for Montrose, to go to the Customs Office. There, he released his wrath on his son. He gained access to the Shipping Register and struck his son's name from the list of shipmasters. This was quite a punishment to deal out, showing that the "difference," as it was put in the records, must have been very serious.[203]

However, over time, the rift resolved itself, and was forgotten, but unfortunately so was the fact that Robert had scored his son's name out of the register! And, in 1791, this became really important.

In this year, Alexander Gowan was captured by the infamous Press Gang. As a shipmaster he had legal immunity from being pressed, but first he had to prove his status. This should have been simple. But when Robert Gowan heard of his son's

---

[196] CE53/1/14

[197] W. Thom, *Parish of Inverbervie or Bervie*, in Sir John Sinclair (ed.) *Old Statistical Account of Scotland*, Volume XIV – Kincardineshire and South and West Aberdeenshire (1982 reprint) 136-147 at 142

[198] *Ibid*

[199] *Ibid*

[200] R. Gowans, *Op. cit.*

[201] W. Thom, *Parish of Inverbervie or Bervie*, in Sir John Sinclair (ed.) *Old Statistical Account of Scotland*, Volume XIV – Kincardineshire and South and West Aberdeenshire (1982 reprint) 136-147 at 142

[202] D. Dobson, *Op. cit.*

[203] CE53/1/14

fate, he knew that he had to act very quickly, remembering with horror his actions of a few years before.

A certificate was sent from Montrose, confirming Alexander's identity as the Master of the *Ann*, to Mr. Playfair, agent for Sir George Howie, Regulating Captain at Leith, but to his astonishment the name "Alexander Gowan" was written in a different hand to the rest of the certificate. Even more puzzling, to him, than the name having been entered in this new hand, was that the name having been previously entered in the same handwriting as the rest of the names of the certificate, now had a dark score through it! Thus he sent the certificate back to Montrose, requesting an explanation, while Gowan remained a detainee. The Collector was baffled![204]

Finally, seeing no other option, Robert Gowan came forward with the truth. After his son had been pressed he, in desperation, had secretly returned to the Customs Office and had his son's name re-inserted on the Registry Certificate – hence Mr. Playfair's confusion as to the change in hand-writing! (It seems likely that Robert in fact sent one of his sons to have the name re-inserted – we know that Robert himself was barely literate, only able to make his own mark "R G."[205]) Robert requested that the certificate be re-issued, and meanwhile his son was released. But by now the whole thing was out of hand, and the complexities of the case necessitated a hearing before the Sheriff-Depute of Kincardine at Stonehaven. In the end, the certificate was re-issued,[206] but not before the Gowans paid the legal fees for the case of £1/0/3, including £0/10/6 for the "Procurator Fiscal's trouble."[207] It had been an expensive argument! Anne Gowan, grand-daughter of Alexander, later recalled an old family saying – *"dinna mak' a man o' them afore their time."* Perhaps this saying had originated for the Gowans with the case of the argument of the young Alexander Gowan with his father, which turned out to be so costly!

After this episode, trade continued very much as it had done for the Gowans and the others in the village, with one exception. As Thom put it, the "ruinous and baneful" trade of smuggling was "much on the decline."[208] This was down to one man – William Blews, from Johnshaven, a remarkable employee of the Montrose Collector.[209] The collector realised that he needed, and so employed, someone who was not mixed up in Gourdon society but who knew the smuggling trade and who was local enough to the area not to earn the immediate hostility of the Gourdon people. In short, a Tidesman who could "merge" better with the locals! As Frances Wilkins put it, in him "at last the smugglers in the Gourdon area had met their match!"[210]

Perhaps partly because of this, and partly because he was by now an old man, in 1790 James Gowan decided to sell his ship, also, rather confusingly, named the *Ann* of Gourdon (this boat was definitely not the same as that that belonged to his brother Robert). I recently found the original contract for the sale of this boat, signed by both James and his son (one of the witnesses) also called James. The contract is dated 18th May 1790, and it was entered into by James Gowan and the purchaser, Alexander Alexander (from Catterline) at the Mill of Catterline. The boat was to be sold *"with her whole Sails... and other [sic] furnitur."* Alexander was to pay £56 in

---

[204] *Ibid*

[205] NAS Ref. SC5/8/116

[206] CE53/1/14

[207] CE53/2/14

[208] W. Thom, *Parish of Inverbervie or Bervie*, in Sir John Sinclair (ed.) *Old Statistical Account of Scotland*, Volume XIV – Kincardineshire and South and West Aberdeenshire (1982 reprint) 136-147 at 138

[209] F. Wilkins, *Op. cit.* p. 151-152

[210] *Ibid* p. 152

installments for the boat, the first installment to be worth £24 and to be paid within eight days of the making of the contract. However, the contract is not very well worded, and one can understand how it gave rise to litigation. It was not clear from the contract whether Alexander was to pay for the boat before it was to be delivered to him or whether he could take delivery of it before the payment of the first installment. Therefore, on the 19th May 1790, this problem became apparent. Alexander and his crew of two (which gives us some idea of the size of the boat) went down to Gourdon from Catterline that day to take the boat back up to Catterline. And at this stage the dispute arose. Gowan later insisted that Alexander offered no payment for the boat, and even stated that he would not be able to pay for it within eight days, but that he simply came to take delivery of it. Alexander claimed that he had offered payment, but that Gowan had simply gone back on his word, and refused to hand over the boat. Gowan clearly did not trust Alexander, because when Alexander tried to seize the boat anyway, he found that Gowan had taken the precaution of removing the "cabal [sic] rope," an essential part of the equipment of the boat, and so it was useless to him. Infuriated, Alexander sent his crew home and went to the "alehouse" in Bervie, perhaps to drown his sorrows. According to Alexander, Gowan then went after him and offered him the boat again in the evening if Alexander would return to Gourdon to take delivery the following day (the 20th). Gowan was silent on this point. Alexander agreed, and returned to Gourdon with his crew the next day, but again Gowan refused to hand over the boat (one might presume because, once again, Alexander failed to come up with any money). Gowan even went to the extent of sending his son out to sea in the boat, to carry on trading in lime as the family had done before. The eight days elapsed without any payment being made to Gowan. So began the legal battle, which dragged on for years, and it is not entirely clear, at this stage, who won. In the short term, from a practical perspective, Gowan won, because he made a reasonable profit out of his activities in this period! On July 3rd 1790, the parties did meet again, and once again Alexander was unable to hand over the money, but Gowan agreed to accept £23 in payment. Gowan's lawyer, George Milne, was later keen to view the two transactions as entirely separate - this helped Gowan as it meant that, if he had been able to withdraw from ("rescind") the earlier contract, due to Alexander's repudiation thereof due to his failure to pay within the eight days, then Gowan could not be sued. Alexander had tried to sue him for breach of the original contract of May 18th 1790. It also meant that the trade profits made between May 18th and July 3rd by Gowan by using his boat could not possibly be claimed as damages by Alexander – he hoped to claim these from Gowan for the use of "his" boat. The value of the trade profits, as alleged by Alexander, was eight pounds sterling from only two journeys. Such large profits may help to explain the rising standards of living experienced by the whole Gowan family in this period – for example, the ability of Robert Gowan (b. 1731) to take more than one lease in Gourdon.

While more research needs to be done into the ultimate outcome of the case, it is clear that things did not go at all well for Alexander. Gowan delayed delivery again, according to Alexander, and when he finally did get the boat it was still without its cable rope and was, in fact, no longer seaworthy! When summoned, the Gowans repeatedly failed to appear before the Sheriff Depute at Stonehaven. But, in defence of the Gowans, it must be noted that Alexander hardly behaved well either during the whole episode. He actually went to the extent of writing in a clause in the original contract, as demonstrated by Gowan's lawyer, to make his case stronger. As Milne put it, "Happy is it for mankind that such bare-faced tricks generally expose themselves!"[211]

Trade carried on into the 1790s, even though some of the traders went further afield to work in other occupations. For example, during his trading days, Alexander Gowan expanded his father's business, even having another sloop built – the Countess of Elgin.[212] The name of this boat betrays the trading activities of the family in this period. Alexander traded for coal that he would sell on in Gourdon. The coal came from areas owned by the Earl of Elgin, and so, presumably, Gowan named his boat after the wife of the man who owned the lands where he made his money. I cannot think of any other reason why the Gowans would call a boat the "Countess of Elgin." It is possible that they bought the coal direct from the Earl, as in the early nineteenth century, James Gowan, probably Alexander's brother, was sued for a debt in the Montrose courts by Mr. Wotherspoon, factor to the Earl.

Later, Alexander is said to have become a deep-water fisherman, apparently sailing as far as the American Colonies.[213] He certainly seems to have sold both his boats towards the end of the first decade of the nineteenth century. He and his wife, Helen Kemlo,[214] had a very large family, and one of his sons, Robert, (b. 1801), even went on to work as a whaler.[215] While the lean years for the fishing lasted, other occupations like these were necessary.

And the Gourdon folk did succeed in them. When he died in 1800, James Gowan, probably brother of Robert Gowan, owner of the *Ann* of Gourdon, left a will[216] – a feat in itself for the Gourdon people (see Appendix One), – and in that will it was noted that he left to his sons and daughters fifty pounds sterling – and that was only what he had with the Aberdeen Banking Company! The fact that he had loose capital like this to invest shows he was fairly comfortable when he died. This cannot have been money from fishing – Thom stated that by 1792 the fishermen earned *"but a scanty pittance."*[217] It must have come from trade – money his sons invested into becoming among the first to buy their own homes in Gourdon.[218]

This was the real legacy of trade in eighteenth century Gourdon - an opportunity for the people of the village to make some money that could be used to help them to get on in life, and then to take some of the opportunities offered by the nineteenth and twentieth centuries. But the market economy was tempered by the circumstances of the people, who were fully aware that with one stroke the sea could make or break their fortunes.

As well as this, the constant smuggling can be seen in the context of the wider protest of the day against impositions of the Hanoverian Government. When taken with the evidence of the stormy relationships involving Gourdon and the Kirk in the next chapter, and Gourdon and the law in the chapter following this, the smuggling becomes significant as part of a picture of a protest which was sweeping the nation in this period.

---

[211] NAS Ref. SC5/8/135

[212] CE53/1/14-18

[213] R. Gowans, *Op. cit.*

[214] Marriage Register of St James the Great Episcopalian Church, Stonehaven

[215] R. Gowans, *Op. cit.*; tradition recalled by Jessie Smith Christie (nee Moncur) 1904-1982

[216] NAS Ref. CC20/4/28

[217] W. Thom, *Parish of Inverbervie or Bervie*, in Sir John Sinclair (ed.) *Old Statistical Account of Scotland,* Volume XIV – Kincardineshire and South and West Aberdeenshire (1982 reprint) 136-147 at 142

[218] Register of Sasines (Kincardineshire) 1780 – 1820 (in the NAS); Bervie Cess Book (at Bervie Library)

CHAPTER FOUR:
THE KIRK AND THE VILLAGE

*"There may be a few dissenters in the parish, but they
are not natives."*[219]

The people of the village of Gourdon often had a very difficult relationship with the Kirk. Right from the start of the records, a picture emerges of conflict between minister (and occasionally Session) and people. At times this aspect of the community's history tells of something approximating (to our eyes, at least) oppression at the hands of the minister. However, the villagers never simply accepted this - on several occasions they fought back, once violently, against the established order. One has to be clear, however, about what, on these occasions, the people of the village were fighting against – not against Christianity itself, but rather the system of discipline that at times they appear to have considered unjust. This is a deeply intriguing tale and much of this chapter will deal with it.

It has to be said, however, that there was real humanity to the Kirk as well. Poor relief was frequently given out, and when those who were in desperate poverty could not even clothe themselves, the Kirk would assist. The expenses following death of buying coffins of poorer people were also often met by the Session. This shall be dealt with towards the end of the chapter, alongside the growing systems of education and even primitive healthcare, encouraged by the Session towards the end of the eighteenth century.

Section One: Minister, Discipline and Session

Little information has survived regarding Gourdon in the pre-Reformation period. People would have worshipped at the old medieval church at Bervie, which survived until the late eighteenth century and which was dedicated to the Blessed Virgin Mary. Aside from this, the village probably came under a very strong Roman Catholic influence due to its proximity to the Carmelite Friary at Bervie, which would have endured until 1567, when the Earl of Moray destroyed the Friary (and much of Bervie with it – Gourdon itself may not have escaped the destruction) as part of his drive to purge the North East of Catholicism. In Bervie his tactics worked – the faith in this form did not re-emerge in the parish for centuries.[220]

It was the following year (it is unlikely that this is a coincidence) that the first reference to a Reformed preacher is found at Bervie – James Symson.[221] He was merely a "Reader" – Bervie Parish was incorporated after the Reformation into one vast parish, along with Garvock, Kinneff, Catterline and Arbuthnott. The unenviable task of administering to this vast flock was given to Rev. Alexander Keith.[222] Of him little is known, except that he came to a bad end, being "slain" on 5th June 1594. It

---

[219] W. Thom, *Parish of Inverbervie or Bervie*, in Sir John Sinclair (ed.) *Old Statistical Account of Scotland*, Volume XIV – Kincardineshire and South and West Aberdeenshire (1982 reprint) 136-147 at 146

[220] R. Souter (ed.) *Gourdon and the Surrounding Area – A Compilation of Information and Essays on Local History (unpublished)*

[221] H. Scott D.D., *Fasti Ecclesiae Scoticanae: Synods of Fife, and of Angus and Mearns* (New Edition 1925) Volume V at 457-458

[222] *Ibid*

was not a good start to the post-Reformation era, and his successors were to fare only slightly better as the years progressed.

Meanwhile, by 1589, the new Bervie Reader was David Rattray, from Slains, who then was moved to Philorth in 1593. His heir was James Rait, who came from Auldearn in 1591, and then was posted to Catterline on 8th June 1613.[223] By now, there were real arguments emerging that Bervie should have its own minister. It was a thriving, growing community, with the port of Gourdon also needing a minister. It was inconvenient for the people of Gourdon and Bervie to travel to the Kirk at Kinneff. In 1613, the minister at Kinneff finally agreed to the appointment of a junior minister at Bervie – Mr. Andrew Moncur MA,[224] who had graduated from Aberdeen in the same year. He may have been a member of the once powerful but by this stage rapidly declining, Moncur family of Slains, whose seat was in Kinneff Parish, and the sale of whose heartlands of Slains and Fawside he witnessed in 1620.[225] In 1622, he witnessed another event – possibly one he helped to instigate. This was somewhat more significant in the history of the county – the creation of Bervie as a separate parish. So, while almost nothing is known about him, it was with Andrew Moncur that the post-Reformation history of Bervie really began.

It was in the time of his heir, Rev. James Strachan, that the earliest surviving minute book of Kirk Session, commencing in 1641, was kept.[226] Sadly, these records are fragmentary, possibly due to the fact that Strachan had other problems. The Civil War was raging, and it was all too easy to end up on the wrong side of the religious disputes of the day. Strachan clung on for eight years after this, but finally fell foul of the General Assembly in October 1649, and was deposed,[227] being replaced with the Rev. William Wright. However, Strachan remained in Bervie, much to Wright's annoyance, and he frequently preached to those of a dissenting nature in the parish. In the end, in the 1660s, the Archbishop of St Andrews put a stop to his sermons for good, and Strachan disappeared from history.

Apart from this, Rev. Wright seems to have seen great merit in fast days, as the records are littered with them in the 1650s.[228] It has to be remembered, however, that he was living in a time when there was so much strife under Cromwell that people were desperate for any remedy to salvage the situation. This would seem to have spread to Bervie Parish.

However, Rev. Wright did make another impact on the parish. It is in the records of his stewardship that reference is first found to Elders from Gourdon – William Burness and William Jaffrey.[229] Although these first recorded Elders were probably of the farm folk of Gourdon, (Jaffrey certainly was[230]) it was the beginning of a new type of administration for the area, where the minister would have an Elder for each part of the parish to act as an intermediary between him and his flock. This was not a new idea even in Kincardineshire, never mind Scotland, but it does seem to have been the earliest recorded instance of it in Bervie.

---

[223] *Ibid*

[224] *Ibid*

[225] NAS Ref. GD49/399. There is an unproven possibility that the later Moncurs of the Mearns, including the Moncurs in Gourdon, descended from junior branches of the Slains and Fawside family. Work is still progressing on this point.

[226] NAS Ref. CH2/34/9-10

[227] H. Scott D.D., *Fasti Ecclesiae Scoticanae: Synods of Fife, and of Angus and Mearns* (New Edition 1925) Volume V at 457-458

[228] NAS Ref. CH2/34/9

[229] *Ibid*

[230] NAS Ref. CC3/3/6, will of probably the same William Jaffrey.

In spite of this reform, which might seem like an attempt to take greater control of his people, Rev. Wright was not particularly heavy-handed with his flock. There is only one record of discipline exercised against the people of Gourdon during his time – on 21ˢᵗ June 1656, Thomas and John Mearns, fishers in Gourdon, and also brothers, were rebuked for fighting in public.[231] And of course one could not expect Rev. Wright to let this pass.

However, his leniency did not last forever. Wright died on 27ᵗʰ August 1669. His heir, William Chalmers,[232] was only slightly less lenient, taking careful note when people missed his sermon, as in 1671, when Alexander Gowan in Gourdon (husband of Marjorie Mearns) "was rebuked befor the congregation," for being at sea while the sermon was going on.[233] However even these disciplinary sessions were rare.

But on 15ᵗʰ April 1674 something happened that really did seriously damage the relationship between people and clergy. The death of William Chalmers was met with the appointment of Peter Rait, from Angus, as the new minister.[234] He was the strictest of all the ministers of Bervie in the implementation of discipline, and it seems that the villagers did not thank him for it.

From the start, Rait was out to enforce a rigorous code of conduct amongst the villagers. He began on July 12ᵗʰ 1674, when Andrew Garvie and John McMaire (presumably in Gourdon) were *delaited for fishing on the Sabbath.*"[235] On September 6ᵗʰ, Margaret Napier in Gourdon, who had *"knocked beare (barley)"* on the Sabbath was rebuked, as was the first known Gourdon fishcurer, Helspit (Elspet) Dorrit, who sold fish on the Sabbath. On June 25ᵗʰ, David Fatt, Robert Gowan, Katherine Allan (Robert's wife) and George Mearns, all in Gourdon were "lawfully charged" of *"sclandoring, flyteing and cursing,"* and ordered to stand before the Session in repentance. Robert Gowan denied the charge and was found to be "not faultie," but Rait seems to have gone back on his word and made him appear anyway in repentance with the others, even though he had committed no misdemeanour (this seems strange, but the records attest both Gowan's innocence and the fact that he was publicly rebuked).[236] On August 8ᵗʰ 1675, Rait and the Session chose to act on information that one woman in Gourdon had been guilty of a real "travesty" – she had been "sewing on the Sabbath" – presumably she was making some clothes for her unborn child which was due very shortly. The minister allowed her some grace to appear to be rebuked for this terrible crime as she was "near her doune lying," (i.e. near to giving birth).[237] By now most of the more belligerent Gourdon families – the Gowans and the Fatts being amongst them – had suffered at Rait's hands. They had been humiliated for minor breaches of discipline and were not likely to forget this treatment.

In July 1676 David Fatt was found guilty of baiting his lines on the Sabbath and rebuked.[238] The appointment of a new Gourdon Elder – this time a fisherman, Thomas Mearns – seems to have made little difference to the mood of the people. It

---

[231] NAS Ref. CH2/34/10

[232] H. Scott D.D., *Fasti Ecclesiae Scoticanae: Synods of Fife, and of Angus and Mearns* (New Edition 1925) Volume V at 457-458

[233] NAS Ref. CH2/34/11/14

[234] H. Scott D.D., *Fasti Ecclesiae Scoticanae: Synods of Fife, and of Angus and Mearns* (New Edition 1925) Volume V at 457-458

[235] NAS Ref. CH2/34/11

[236] *Ibid*

[237] *Ibid*

[238] *Ibid*

is possible that this was a catalyst for the rather unorthodox form of protest that followed which was embarked upon by the villagers.

Peter Rait seems to have taken to having a roll call of his parishioners on a Sunday to make sure that they were all present. Imagine, then, his shock on entering the Kirk at Bervie on Sunday 20th August 1676, to find that hardly a single soul from Gourdon had appeared to hear his sermon.[239] Now this is rather remarkable. What had happened to prevent the people of the village from attending the kirk? All that the records tell is that, over the next few weeks, the villagers trickled back to the church and were rebuked as they came. Given the circumstances of the time, it seems to me that the only possible explanation for this sequence of events – the refusal to attend followed by the rebukes - must lie in some concerted protest on the part of the villagers against the discipline of the Session. Perhaps the villagers felt that Rait was in some way acting unjustly in relation to them. Obviously it does not take much imagination to understand that individuals could dislike disciplinarian measures taken in relation to them. But before a whole community would react in this fashion one has to perceive that Rait had either alienated the whole village in some way or that he was perceived to have acted unjustly in relation to so many individuals in the village that they decided to react by virtually "boycotting" his sermon. We cannot be sure what caused this; but a connection with the strict discipline enforced by Rait appears plausible. But whatever caused this action, it persisted amongst some of the villagers for a whole month, until September 10th – quite remarkable in this period. It is dangerous to read too much into this episode; but it does seem to constitute a very early form of popular protest.

In any event, Rev. Rait continued to exert discipline over the people of Gourdon. On October 29th 1676 David Law and his wife sold drink to beggars on Sunday, which caused them to be rebuked.[240] On 13th May 1677 Nicholas Paton and Mary Mearns were convicted of going home before the "Afternoon Service" began.[241]

Some of the actions of the Gourdon people seem to have almost been designed to annoy Rait. On July 14th 1678 Andrew Jamie, David Jamie and Thomas Fatt stayed away from the Kirk and started to drink alcohol back in Gourdon while the sermon was going on. Their penance was to stand before the Session to be rebuked in "wheet sheets," (presumably something like sackcloth).[242] But eventually the situation began to ease. Occurrences of breaches of discipline lessened. It is unclear what caused this – perhaps the villagers decided to be more co-operative with Rait; perhaps he decided to be more lenient with them. However, I would be unwilling to make too much of the August 1676 incident in attempting to understand this apparent change.

The years of the 1680s were marked by religious troubles for the Scots. Charles II repeatedly sought to assert the power of the Crown over that of the Kirk and he met with stiff resistance in Scotland, in particular from the radical Covenanters. And these troubles did touch Kincardineshire. In 1685, at the height of the Killing Times, many Covenanters were rounded up and imprisoned in various locations. According to the *"Black Book of Kincardineshire,"* a large number of them were imprisoned in Dunnottar Castle. They remained loyal to their principles, as did the majority of Covenanters. The survivors of the dungeon were finally deported to America. Seventy died on the voyage.

---

[239] *Ibid*
[240] *Ibid*
[241] *Ibid*
[242] *Ibid*

It would be rather difficult to lay out here all of the confusing troubles that faced Scots Christianity in the 1680s. One was not dealing with a simple matter of Presbyterian Scots confronting Episcopalian and Catholic Scots; moderate Presbyterians shunned their radical counterparts, in the hope of ensuring the survival of a Presbyterian system under Charles II. But even the moderates were often unable to comply with the requirements of Charles II. This led, for many, to imprisonment or exile. These were troubled times. For example, James Dalrymple of Stair himself, now hailed as the father of Scots Law, was forced to flee on a point of principle to Holland during this period, due to the fact that he refused to take the oath asserting royal supremacy over the Kirk. In 1685, Charles II died; and he was succeeded by his Catholic brother, James VII and II. His reign did not last long. He was deposed in the revolution of 1688-1689, and, shortly afterwards, the Protestant William of Orange became King of England. After the death of Bonnie Dundee, a great Jacobite commander in Scotland, William was militarily unopposed in Lowland Scotland, on the condition that he would restore the Presbyterian Church as the Established Church of Scotland.

All of this confusion, which, unfortunately, is generally not commented upon in the Kirk Session records, touched Bervie. Peter Rait, who was a man of principle – whatever one might say about the rest of his actions, one must at least give him credit for standing by his beliefs – refused to pray for William of Orange or to read the Proclamation of the Estates on the matter. In short, he was probably a Jacobite, like so many of his counterparts across the Mearns, who were also Episcopalian. By 1695 the Privy Council had tired of Rait. They deposed him as a minister, and he died three years later, in October 1698, aged fifty-six.[243] Interestingly, unlike some of his counterparts, Rait was either unwilling or unable to lead any of his parishioners away from the Kirk – many of the other deposed ministers in the Mearns, who were Episcopalian, did. Perhaps Rait did not command the necessary loyalty amongst his following for this to happen – as it did in most of the other parishes in Kincardinshire, certainly in the north of the county.

The new minister was Rev. James Arbuthnott, who was a brother of a Baillie of Montrose.[244] No records of discipline survive from his time, but his stewardship saw some of the most important changes in Church History in Scotland. In 1707, of course, the Union of the Parliaments occurred (not even hinted at in the minutes of the time!) and this was the direct precursor to three vital decisions that came from the Houses of Parliament in 1712. Firstly, a decision of the House of Lords in that year effectively legalised Episcopalianism (within rather strict constraints) – this was not directly important in Bervie. Secondly, the power of the Kirk to support lesser excommunication (withdrawal of communion), with the ability to pursue a civil case against the defenders when the issue arose, was removed. Thirdly, the right of the people to elect their ministers was removed. In the immediate future, this last provision seems to have caused the most trouble in Gourdon, and throughout Scotland. Seldom, however, were the troubles as violent as in this North-East village.

In 1713 Rev. Arbuthnott became the third of the past six ministers of Bervie to be deposed, in his case, for *"disrespect of the Sabbath."*[245] At least Rait would have been pleased to see his favourite cause to bring discipline applied to all levels of

---

[243] H. Scott D.D., *Fasti Ecclesiae Scoticanae: Synods of Fife, and of Angus and Mearns* (New Edition 1925) Volume V at 457-458
[244] *Ibid*
[245] *Ibid*

society in the parish! But his heir was to be "presented," not elected, and the Bervie people, in particular those in Gourdon, were not to accept this lightly!

The unfortunate man chosen to succeed Arbuthnott was Rev. William Arnott. He was due to be ordained at Bervie on 19th May 1714, but was shocked to discover that, once again, the people of the parish had taken matters into their own hands. Many were inside the kirk building, which had been turned into a virtual fortress against the incoming incumbent, the "doors and windows barricaded," and although he and the other dignitaries involved in the ordination did their best to break in, they failed. Beaten, they retreated to Benholm. Some may have thought this was victory. The Gourdon people thought differently. Having been ordained at Benholm, the furious Rev. Arnott resolved at once to confront the troublesome flock at Bervie, probably against the better judgement of others present. The people were in no mood to accept a minister they had had no part in appointing!

As he was thundering on his horse along the road to Bervie, suddenly some of the Gourdon men leapt out from the evening shadows and seized the minister, dragging him from his horse, another remarkably bold move, even more astonishing and daring than the protests of 1676. Amid his fury Arnott was led into Gourdon where he was imprisoned, for a while, in one of the Victual Houses in the village. While he nursed his wrath, the people decided that it wasn't safe to keep him in Gourdon. Quickly they removed the minister and took him to a house outwith the parish. There they held him for some time!

Eventually the Presbytery got wind of this disturbance and sent a delegation to release Arnott. Having heard the request, the Gourdon people still refused to let the minister go, and finally the Presbytery tried force. Even this failed at first, and the Gourdon folk *"violently repulsed them with many indignities!"* Finally, however, when they could hold out no longer, they were forced grudgingly to release Arnott.[246] But he was still placed in charge of the parish. However, once again the Gourdon folk had made their voices heard.

Yet Rev. Arnott did not take any sort of revenge on the people after this episode, and he may even have had more of a will to ally with the people of Gourdon rather than to always clamp down on them – showing some strength of character in light of his earlier experience!

Throughout the early years of Arnott's ministry in Bervie there is little record of discipline – that said, the records available are not particularly detailed in this period. However, in the early 1720s, this changed – possibly a new Session Clerk was appointed.[247] Even this change sadly did not result in some of the most important events in the history of the parish being noted, such as the admittance of elders to the Session. But it would seem that Thomas Mearns had long since died, and Gourdon was without an elder. Then, in about 1730, Arnott decided on a new policy, to be followed by his successors – to revive the old idea of an elder to "look after" Gourdon, but to add to it by bringing more of the villagers on to the Session. Whether the policy was designed to "build bridges" cannot be gleaned from the records, but what is certain is that Arnott pursued it with a great deal of determination.

The first man he asked to be a new elder was Robert Mearns, who was probably kith or kin to most of the village. This certainly did not make Mearns's task easy!

---

246 *Ibid*
247 NAS Ref. CH2/34/14

The villagers very quickly started making their complaints to Mearns. On November 8[248] 1730, Margaret Annan went to him for help because she was "with child," and the man she said was the father, Robert Clark, servant to Robert Dickie in Gourdon, was refusing to have anything to do with her.[248] However, on this occasion, the Session, having questioned Annan, found her to be *"grossly ignorant,"* casting doubt on her testimony, decided to accquit the man accused of fatherhood. The Session gave her no more help, once, of course, she had been thoroughly "rebuked."

One particular case stands out in the 1730s from the records[249] – that of a fearsome matriarch of the Gourdon Mearns family, who by birth belonged to the Gowan tribe. She was Agnes Gowan. She may have been the same as the Agnes born in 1674, daughter of Robert Gowan and Catherine Allan.[250] It is tempting to suggest that she may have also been the Agnes who married Robert Mearns in 1696 in Kineff and Catterline.

One day in late September 1732, Janet Allan, sister of David Allan, fisher in Gourdon,[251] had the misfortune of crossing Agnes's path. One can almost picture the scene, as Agnes made some off-hand remark to Janet by the harbour at Gourdon, and then Janet (not being one to allow the remark to just pass!) retaliating as best she could. After a few minutes of these exchanges, (the two women, like those Burns knew, nursing their wrath to keep it warm), the clamour began to attract others to the scene. By the time John Hodge, Robert Gibb Younger, Anna Criggie and George Gove's wife had arrived, something clearly had to be done. David Allan came out to defend his sister, just in time to hear the roar of anathema that Gowan let loose, yelling, ever one for spectacle, that Janet was a "brazen faced bitch!" Having followed this with other curses and *"opprobrious language,"* as David Allan put it, someone finally intervened before either Allan or Gowan struck the first blow. As Janet was dragged away by her enraged brother, Agnes, not being the sort just to let a matter drop, bellowed after her that she would *"cause her to leave the town!"*

The Allans, however, were not going to tolerate this behaviour. After the service on October 1st of that year, David Allan went to the Session, complaining that Agnes Gowan had "abused his family by cursing [and] swearing." The members of the Session ordered Agnes to appear before them the following Sunday. All those present that day of the confrontation were also ordered to come before the Session to give evidence. As stated above, Arnott had already had some serious problems with Gourdon and he must have groaned as, the following Sunday, yet again the Gourdon folk filed in in front of him.

In remarkable detail David Allan reported to the Session all of the goings on, having brought all the witnesses that he had first cited, as well as another, Margaret Law, for good measure. Not intimidated, Agnes Gowan seems to have seen no reason to deny the charge, still certain that she was in the right!

Just as the Session didn't think this little *"widow woman"* could get any worse, Anna Criggie made another complaint against her. Tired of being called a *"bitch,"* and of her husband, John Criggie, being called an *"Ancient cheat"* by Agnes, she angrily told the Session of how this woman had *"prayed evil prayers unprecotious to her and her family."*[252] Anna Criggie was then asked by Arnott why she hadn't told the Session of this before. The reply was blunt – Agnes was her aunt!

[248] *Ibid*
[249] NAS Ref. CH2/34/14/38-42
[250] Bervie OPRs NAS Ref. RD 254
[251] NAS Ref. CH2/34/14/38-42
[252] *Ibid*

By now astonished at the whole business, the Session, perhaps in fear itself of Gowan, decided to be lenient, and did not discipline her in public. Instead she was *"rebuked"* and *"seriously dealt with."* Ending on an optimistic note, the Session *"exhorted her to a more Christian way in time coming."* The Allans must have been furious at this leniency.

Two weeks later, Jean Watt, spouse to Thomas Blews in Gourdon, brought another complaint before the Session against Gowan, along with her son John Mearns and his wife Margaret Largie. Apparently, the three had declared that Jean Watt was:

> *"a Thief, a whore damned whore and said she*
> *was come of whores of thieves."*[253]

But Watt's evidence is suspect. Her witnesses were David Allan and John Criggie (the "Ancient cheat,") Agnes's niece's husband. Both had good reason to fabricate evidence against Gowan, especially after the Kirk had, in their view, perhaps, failed to discipline her as was her *"due."* No one else witnessed these *"imprecations"* against Watt, and the Blews family, being from Johnshaven like the Criggies and the Allans, might have been "allies" of that camp. This time too Agnes and her son denied the charges against them – not a repeat of her earlier display of defiance, which perhaps implies that the charges were not true. But the Session, wanting to put an end to the affair, made Agnes and her son satisfy Kirk Discipline. They were *"rebuked publically before the congregation,"* and had to *"pay a penaltie,"* for the breach of conduct. It seems tempting to argue that the Allans and the Criggies had engineered the justice they wanted. Perhaps the Session had been too lenient, but it might be argued that this was an instance of how the Parish State could be used to "settle scores."

The Parish State could also, by its very nature, cause great pain to innocent individuals. On November 5th, 1732, James Milne, fisher in Gourdon, spoke to Rev. Arnott after the Sunday Sermon. His wife, Margaret Allan, had recently given birth, and, naturally, they wanted the child to baptised. But there was a problem. The minister checked up on Milne and his wife, and discovered that they had only been married seven months before the child was born. This raised the question of "antenuptial fornication," one which the Session pursued, even though they knew full well that the child could simply have been premature. This was what Milne insisted – life must have been hard enough for him at the time without this investigation. He was ordered to produce evidence, if he could, that, when the child was born, it was "imperfect" – i.e. premature. So he had to return to Gourdon to find those present at the birth – Jane Grieg, the village midwife, Christian Scott, wife of John Hodge and Isabel Gove, wife of David Allan. They confirmed that the child had been "imperfect," and that Milne and his wife were innocent.[254] Accordingly they were acquitted, but the unnecessary stress (and fear that the child could die before it was baptised, a real fear in the case of a premature baby and one which would have deeply affected any eighteenth century member of the Kirk) must have left a feeling of anti-clerical resentment in the village, reviving the old troubles of 1676 and 1714. This may help to explain why, in part, Robert Mearns the Kirk Elder reported *"cursing and swearing"* directed at him and his family by Elspeth Cormak in Gourdon.[255] Of course it may be purely co-incidental, but the mood of the village was turning once

---

[253] *Ibid*
[254] NAS Ref. CH2/34/14
[255] *Ibid*

again against the institution of the Kirk at Bervie. The case of John Gowan in 1740 may be another example of this.

John Gowan, alias Jock, was one of the few villagers fortunate enough not have fallen foul of the minister or the Session at some time or another. He was probably the same man as the Jock Gowan mentioned in Chapter Three above, the earliest ancestor of the Gowan family recalled by the oral tradition. (See Appendix Five.) He may have been the keeper of the Shore Inn, and while there is no written evidence surviving to confirm this, the strength of the oral tradition about him does support this assertion.[256] He married in 1725 and had four sons and perhaps a daughter,[257] and when his father died he probably inherited one of his three sloops (according to tradition.[258]) As such he was, locally, a man of some standing in the village. He was the sort of person Arnott wanted on his side.

So, in 1740, the minister, always looking for new elders, approached John Gowan and another Gourdon fisher, Robert Walsh, to ask them to join the Session. He made his request on February 23rd, and was frustrated in that neither gave any answer until June 1st, when Walsh finally agreed to join the Session. However, the minister had less luck with Gowan:-

"The minister reports that he has again spoken wt..
John Gowan who has taken some time to deliberate. The Minister
Applied to gett his answer at the next meeting.."[259]

This begs the question as to why Gowan was deliberating over whether or not to become an elder. There were several good reasons to be concerned about such an appointment. Firstly, to be the village Elder in these times was to earn the contempt of many of the people there, most of them family. Secondly, by now Gowan was one of the more senior members of his family – he may have thought it wrong that he should have to "clipe" on his own relatives. Thirdly, he had grown up in an atmosphere of hostility towards Arnott – why should he now support him? Finally, he was not a young man – he was probably about fifty, and the role of elder was a challenging one. Probably all of these reasons contributed to his turning down the offer by June 8th 1740. But once again this was an intriguing situation, showing at least that there was a shrewdness to Gowan, and doubtless to others in the village, but also, if the above deductions concerning Gowan's rejection of the office are correct, a somewhat principled nature to the man. A decision to refuse the parochial prestige of being an elder was not lightly made, and whatever else one might say, Gowan certainly gave it a lot of thought!

The following year saw the end of an era. In 1741, William Arnott became the first minister of Bervie in seventy-one years not to be deposed. He died peacefully on September 20th, the longest serving minister of Bervie as a parish in its own right since before the Reformation. This was no mean achievement for someone who had spent his first day in his new parish under lock and key! His heir was Rev. Thomas Dow, who was appointed as minister on 9th December 1741. Another

---

[256] R. Gowans, *The Gowans* (1940s) in R. Souter (ed.) *Gourdon and the Surrounding Area – A Compilation of Information and Essays on Local History (unpublished)*
[257] Bervie OPRs NAS Ref. RD 254
[258] R. Gowans, *Op. cit.*
[259] NAS Ref. CH2/34/1

minister like Arnott in many ways, he was also to be personally responsible for saving the villages of Gourdon and Johnshaven from some degree of destruction.[260]

Ordained on 23rd June 1742, he immediately began to make some changes to the state of record-keeping in the parish. He decided that all of the new records should be bound in a proper ledger,[261] rather than, as had been the case before, in the hap-hazard bundles of paper collected by each Session Clerk, which are fortunate to have survived. It was a sign of things to come – Dow, like Arnott and Rait before him, liked order in his parish. However, it would seem that because of Arnott's more moderate attitude towards the parishioners (when compared to that of Rait), and because the establishment in the parish had got used to the idea of an un-elected minister (however much they may still have disliked it) there was no repetition of the scenes of twenty-nine years before. Dow knew he would have to tread a careful path, but was determined not to allow this to compromise Kirk Discipline.

He started out well. On the fifth of June 1743 there were *"very great profanations of the Lord's Day committed by the fishers in Gourdon."* It turned out that they had been smuggling on the Sabbath. By now Robert Mearns had resigned as an elder, and so new members of the Session were needed for the village. The men chosen were Daniel Watt and Robert Walsh, but, at this stage, both refused to give a firm answer as to whether or not they would accept the office in the long term (probably they had the same reservations about the office as John Gowan had had three years before). Even so, they helped Dow in his investigations about the Sabbath breach. As it happened, the fishermen confessed to going to sea on that particular Sunday. Very calmly Dow agreed to say no more about it – there was to be no public humiliation for the fishers this time round, since they agreed not to act like this on the Sabbath again.

It was to be a full two years after this that the minister finally got his answer from Watt and Walsh. The former declined the office of an elder while the latter accepted, but only if another Gourdon man was appointed to share his "burden!" It seems he thought there was safety in numbers! In response to this Robert Mearns was invited to return to the Session, and did so, with surprising haste.

These troubles were minor, however. Dow's first real test as a minister was completely different. It arose in 1746, towards the end of the last Jacobite Rebellion. While the people of Gourdon, and the neighbouring village of Johnshaven, in Benholm Parish, had played almost no part in the rising, possibly in part due to long memories which recalled the dislike they had felt for the Jacobite Rait, they were still greatly at risk. As Cumberland marched north, he learned that the counties of Angus and Kincardineshire were swarming with Jacobites. Cumberland sought to "remedy" this situation. When a report arrived that the people of Johnshaven had helped the retreating rebels by giving them supplies, he had his excuse. His troops marched on the village, with orders to crush all resistance, and they did, burning and looting in the place, perhaps setting fire to those boats that had not been put to sea quickly enough by their crews. It must have been a terrible scene, as the Redcoats went about their work, and, once the news reached Gourdon, the people there knew that they might be next. Those who could perhaps put to sea with their families, thus at least saving themselves and their livelihoods.

Someone, however, had the sense to go to the one man in the parish who might be willing and able to help – Rev. Dow. It is a measure of the man that,

---

[260] H. Scott D.D., *Fasti Ecclesiae Scoticanae: Synods of Fife, and of Angus and Mearns* (New Edition 1925) Volume V at 457-458
[261] NAS Ref. CH2/34/1

whenever he heard of the plight of the people of Johnshaven, he quickly rode out to meet Cumberland to intercede on their behalf. The act was brave, considering that, in this time, any action made in a bid to stop the Duke in his tracks could be interpreted as treason. Dow did not have diplomatic immunity!

On approaching the soldiers, he was intercepted and brought before Cumberland. Somehow he persuaded the arrogant Duke to see that the people of Benholm and Bervie were of no threat to him. He may have cited the lack of Episcopacy and Catholicism in the parishes to demonstrate the loyalty of the people - those professing Episcopacy or Catholicism would have fallen under strong suspicion of Jacobite sympathy. But whatever Dow did, it worked. Cumberland called off the attack, and Gourdon was spared.[262] Johnshaven was sadly less fortunate, but there are no records of any fatalities resulting from the attack, and the records imply that economic recovery was fairly swift.

Dow also invited Cumberland to stay at the manse in Bervie that evening, which made certain the security of the village of Gourdon.[263] Now, some might say, perhaps, that this was not the most principled course of action, in light of Cumberland's character – but it was one that saved many livelihoods, and perhaps even lives. To say that Dow should not have acted as he did, and in some fashion "made a stand" against the Duke, is Hollywood history. What else could he have done? Had he done nothing, the people might have faced ruin. Had he stood up to Cumberland, condemning his actions more overtly, he would have probably been denounced as a rebel, having lost all opportunity to assist his people. Given the circumstances and the historical context Dow's hospitality to the Duke, while at first seeming perhaps overly pragmatic, is hard to condemn. Indeed, I think that history should praise Dow for his courage in this episode. He put his parishioners' interests before his own – if his attempts to dissuade the Duke from his actions had been interpreted as rebellious, he would have been in serious danger. Doubtless, however, as they saw the invaders coming, the Gourdon folk would have felt a good deal of animosity towards them.

But life went on in the parish. On a final note in relation to the occupation of the parish by the Hanoverians, we do have a rather interesting letter[264] from Viscount Arbuthnott dated August 8th 1746. This was a protest sent to the Earl of Albermarle, Commander in Chief of the government forces in Scotland, by Arbuthnott because of the actions of a rather arrogant officer who was a dragoon of Cobham's Regiment – Lieutenant Draper. Draper was presumably in charge of the government forces in Bervie and Gourdon. He and his dragoons had gone to Arbuthnott House, where they seized from Arbuthnott *"a silver handed sword, two mourning ones, two pair of pistols... and a fouling piece."* This was done in the *"most arbitrary and forceable manner possible."* Draper did not even turn up in person to seize the articles from a man who was one of the most important locals; he sent his sergeant. The sergeant threatened Arbuthnott that if he did not hand over the arms then his mansion house would be burnt down. It is not clear whether or not the Viscount got his weapons back. What one can say is that the people in Gourdon probably also suffered under what would appear to have been a rather petty officer on some sort of a power trip who probably took great pleasure in stamping authority not only on the ordinary locals but on their leaders too.

---

[262] H. Scott D.D., *Fasti Ecclesiae Scoticanae: Synods of Fife, and of Angus and Mearns* (New Edition 1925) Volume V at 457-458
[263] *Ibid*
[264] C. S. Terry, (ed.) *The Albemarle Papers* (1902) Volume II p. 79-80

The Session Clerk certainly does not seem to have viewed all of these troubles as very significant, due to the extreme lack of any details about them in the records! Discipline carried on, much as it had done before,[265] with one exception – the system of using the Testificat, whereby one had to bring a certificate confirming one's good character in a past home before moving to a new one, was probably abandoned, or at least scaled down.[266] Since the record-keeping from 1742 onwards seems to have been properly organised, it is unlikely that, had the Testificat been in use, it would not have been noted when people moved into the parish. It may already have fallen into disuse in Arnott's day, but since the records are somewhat scant in places, this cannot be certain. This implies a shift away from Rait's concept of the degree of authority that the Parish was able to exercise over individuals (Rait certainly employed the Testificat as a means of control[267]).

This aside, discipline did not change much at first. In 1748, Dow showed that his patience with the Sabbath-breaking fishers did have limits. After Robert Freeman, David Criggie, William Alexander, George Gove and James Watt had confessed to staying away from the Kirk, they were forced to satisfy discipline by appearing before the congregation in penance. Dow also sternly warned them that if any of them did this again he would attempt to bring a civil action against the guilty parties.[268]

However, at least one of the Gourdon people acquitted themselves well in Dow's eyes. Robert Mearns became the first fisherman from the village to be chosen to represent the parish as Ruling Elder at the upcoming Synod at Brechin in 1749. As such he must have been considered quite a capable person, and he remained as Ruling Elder for six months, which was the usual time allotted to each elder in the office at Bervie.[269] The blow must have been a great one, then, in late 1749, when he and his family left the parish. Now there was only Robert Walsh to make the will of the Kirk known in the village and it was still no easy task!

After a quiet year in 1750, trouble stirred up again in 1751. On January 6th, David Criggie, Andrew Jeamie, William Jeamie, John Jeamie, Thomas Fatt and James Freeman were accused of going to sea on the Sabbath again. They insisted that they had taken to their boats to help a ship in distress, but this was not how Dow saw the situation. He had lost patience with the fishermen, and was convinced that they had gone to the ship, not to help, but to bring smuggled goods ashore. Whatever the truth, all were *"rebuked before the Session."* However, Dow stopped short of carrying out his threat of bringing a civil action against the men.[270] Attitudes to discipline were beginning to change in many parts of Scotland, and Dow may have been affected by this. Young radicals like Rev. Thomas Gillespie were questioning the Established Church[271] and the value of its structures of absolute control over punishing individual Christians who had gone astray. Dow did not agree; but he did not agree either with the notion that one should pursue every breach of discipline that arose. He also tried to appoint a new village elder on February 15th, Robert Gibb Younger. Unfortunately for the minister, Gibb did not want the dubious honour![272]

[265] NAS Ref. CH2/34/1
[266] *Ibid*
[267] NAS Ref. CH2/34/11
[268] NAS Ref. CH2/34/1/98
[269] NAS Ref. CH2/34/1
[270] NAS Ref. CH2/34/1 (Jan. 6th 1751)
[271] T. M. Devine, *The Scottish Nation 1700-2000* p. 90
[272] NAS Ref. CH2/34/1

After this last incident of Sabbath breach, the vast majority of cases involving the Gourdon people concerned sexual sin, and also the ongoing struggle to get new elders! An example of the former is seen in a long-drawn out battle to get two people to confess to adultery – Robert Freeman and Christian Blews, wife of James Watt, Shipmaster in Gourdon. The case dragged on for weeks, and no fewer than seven witnesses were called (quite a record by Bervie standards – and all claimed to have witnessed the incident in question) – William Jeamie, Andrew Jeamie, Robert Mearns son to John Mearns, Ann Criggie daughter to John Criggie (and possibly great niece of the infamous Agnes Gowan), and Katherine Smith widow of John Jeamie, along with two Customs Officers from Montrose. The case finally went against Blews, who insisted to the end that she was not guilty, in spite of the fact that everyone, including Robert Freeman, said that she was.[273]

Antenuptial fornication also remained an issue the Session would pursue. In January 1755, Ann Criggie (perhaps the same as the person mentioned above) married Robert Gowan, (b. 1731, son of John Gowan). Three months later their first child, John, was born, and Robert went to the Session to ask for the child to be baptised. But while Dow still insisted that Gowan and his wife should satisfy discipline, he did not do what Arnott had done before him, and insist that before the child was baptised discipline should be satisfied. All Gowan had to do was to promise to come before the Kirk Session, and then Dow went to baptise the child.[274] Little compromises like this probably helped to save Dow's ministry from a people who had never been far from dissent in past generations. And the Gourdon people still had not been completely brought under the "wing" of the Kirk – in the same year John Gowan had once again refused to be an elder. Dow had to tread very carefully.

But this he did. In Gourdon he had help again – Robert Mearns and his family had returned, and Mearns was re-appointed as an elder.[275] It was the age of the moderates, and it might be fair to describe Dow as a conservative moderate, who sought to keep what he viewed as essential aspects of discipline strong while not allowing the letter of the law to blind him to potential compromises that he could use to prevent dissent, while at the same time making it clear that the church did seek a particular standard of conduct from its members.

And so, perhaps in part due to this changed attitude to discipline, as the eighteenth century continued, the desperate need for Gourdon elders diminished. Walsh and his family left in 1758,[276] and he was not replaced with someone from the village. Mearns remained an elder until 1773, when, probably because he was fairly old and poor, possibly being among those on the roll of poor for Bervie, he retired.[277]

By far the biggest shock to the parish, however, was the loss, on 17th September 1787, of Rev. Dow, after forty-five years of administering to the flock. His heir was Rev. Robert Croll (1747-1820), who had been the schoolmaster at Bervie for eight years already.[278] As per Dow's legacy, discipline continued to be practised into this new minister's time in Bervie, but in the same more lenient fashion. In 1797, for example, James Gowan, youngest son of Robert Gowan and Ann Criggie, was accused of fathering the illegitimate son of his father's "late servant," Margaret

---

[273] NAS Ref. CH2/34/1/175-176
[274] NAS Ref. CH2/34/1/219-220
[275] NAS Ref. CH2/34/1
[276] *Ibid*
[277] NAS Ref. CH2/34/2; NAS Ref. CH2/34/7
[278] H. Scott D.D., *Fasti Ecclesiae Scoticanae: Synods of Fife, and of Angus and Mearns* (New Edition 1925) Volume V at 457-458

Criggie. Unfortunately for the Session, he was "not at home," and remained as such for some time. It took four years for the Session to finally get him to pay the penalty due. This indicates that the discipline system was very much in decline in the parish.

This section, then, shows that Thom's evaluation of the character of the people of Gourdon, taken in 1792, incorporated a fundamental mistake. There were dissenters in the parish, most of them natives – but the willingness of the people to dissent in the more obvious ways of their ancestors had subsided by the early 1790s. After Arnott was released from imprisonment at the hands of the Gourdon folk there was never again in the period before 1800 dissent such as that witnessed in 1676 and in 1714. Therefore there remains an obvious question. It is true that the discipline system was in decline in the eighteenth century. The impracticalities and partial relaxation of the system may help to account in part for this. But there was more to Dow's reform of the parish – he seems to have attempted to create an embryonic form of parish welfare state, as is shown in the next section of this chapter. Does this in itself help to explain the lack of dissent for such a long period amongst the parishioners? If this is so, the picture is far subtler than one of raving protestors who were gradually appeased by a church repenting of a burdensome system of discipline; and it is also far more complex than Thom's picture of a docile community that essentially refused dissent out of love for conservatism and a refusal to concern itself with matters of religion or politics.

While one might criticise the system of discipline imposed by the Kirk, it must also be remembered that, without the welfare system employed by the Church, primitive as it may have been, the lives of many Scots would have been considerably poorer in quality. This was certainly the case in Gourdon. The Kirk was not just concerned with the hereafter; many ministers also took the view that it was vitally important to raise the quality of life enjoyed by their parishioners in the here and now. It is true that this really began to develop only towards the end of the eighteenth century in the parish of Bervie, but even so there were certainly steps taken before this date that can be seen as contributory to this development. The desire to help all of the parishioners in this manner arose chiefly out of the stress placed by the Reformers on the equality of all souls before God, and therefore the shared rights to education and welfare of all souls. This certainly was the belief in Bervie and Gourdon, and the effects of this on the lives of the people were varied and are deeply intriguing. The most significant, finally, came as the increase of welfare, coinciding with the decrease of enforced discipline, seems to have quietened the voices of anti-clerical protest among the people. To demonstrate how this happened one might focus on poor relief, attempts to better educate the children of the parish and attempts to develop the means available to care for the health of the villagers.

The earliest mention of the people of Gourdon in the registers of the Kirk Session comes with a list of poor, which was recorded in June 1648.[279] From the list, nine of the twenty-five recorded people probably came from the village – Kathren Ritchie, David Meirnes, David Tod, David Jamie, Androw Kermaige (Cormack), Issobell Mearns, James Feascher, Alexander Feascher and Jon Ritchie. Each received twenty shillings Scots, apart from the last three, who received ten shillings. Because the records are not complete at this date it is difficult to tell how frequently the relief was given – in later periods it was distributed to most of the poor monthly or annually,[280] depending on how dire the circumstances of the individuals were. The aid at this stage was purely monetary and was distributed on behalf of the Session by the elder responsible for Gourdon, and was drawn from the weekly collections taken on Sundays, or from interest paid on loans from the Session.

Little changed in the way in which the relief itself was given out until the early eighteenth century. However, it was often well targeted. On February 29th 1648, for example, relief was granted to all of the Gourdon fishermen after a terrible "tempest" had caused them great "distress."[281] Sadly, the pages of the records themselves are incomplete, and so the form that this aid took cannot be discerned. Probably it took a monetary form.

By 1659, of the poor of eleven years before from Gourdon only Issobell Mearns remained. The relief itself remained fixed at twenty shillings per person, but apart from this it is difficult to tell what had spurred the poverty that necessitated it in the first place. Probably not all those whose names appear on the list were included simply because they were too old to work. Individuals disappeared and reappeared from time to time, and even *"marchands"* (merchants) were not immune to sporadic

---

[279] NAS Ref. CH2/34/9
[280] NAS Ref. CH2/34/7
[281] NAS Ref. CH2/34/10

**Old Gourdon
looking towards
Craig David**

**Old Gourdon Harbour
(out of use by 1694)**

**"The Hill" overlooking
Gourdon Harbour**

Ruins of Old Bervie Kirk

Headstone in Bervie Kirkyard

"*Erected by Robert Gowan, Shipmaster in Gurdon and Ann Craigie, his spouse, at the foot whereof lies the body of their daughter, Isabel Gowan ....*"

Dated 1783

Lang Close (left)
Shore Inn (1650's - 1930's)

Probable Site
Of
"Slough of Despond"

Mowatt's Lane
Home of James Mowat
(1735 - 1798)

"The (probable) Hawyning Place Of Gerdoun"
(Mentioned 1549)

The Main Harbour Today

The Main Harbour Today

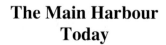

poverty. It seems that relief was given out even at this early date to a variety of people for a variety of reasons.[282]

For the following fifty years, the records mention little change. In the days of Rait discipline took precedence.[283] It was to be one of his successors, Rev. Arnott, who would take a more active role in the way parish support was channelled.

On April 9th 1721, for example, one of the elders, Baillie Beattie, bought *"seven ells and ane half"* of material, to be given to David Jamie and his wife to be made into new clothes for them.[284] The gift was worth £2/5/0, but in this manner the Session ensured that their help went on what they felt the poor really needed. In the same year they did make a gift of £1/0/0 to Jamie again, but specified that this should be used to *"buy a pair of shoes."*

The Session also cared for those whose fathers were lost at sea. The great disaster, known as the "Storm of Wind," (see Chapter Three), left destitute many widows and children – dependents of men drowned in the hurricane. In response to this tragedy, the Kirk Session is known to have put in place long-term help for the victims.[285] For no fewer than twenty-four years the Session continued to help them, until, by 1754, they judged it to be the case that the afflicted were financially self-supporting.

Not only food and clothing were supplied by the Session to the poor – shelter was as well. On June 7th 1752, the Session repaired Isabel Fatt's house in Gourdon at its own expense.[286]

The Session also realised how easily poverty could be brought on, and that they had to react to this. For example, on August 11th 1766, James Mowatt, the newly arrived weaver from Kinneff, (see Chapter Five), and his family, were *"in very indigent circumstances,"* as his wife had *"lately brought forth twins."* It seems that times were hard and the two extra mouths to feed were too much for the weaver to cope with. Mowatt was given £0/8/0 Sterling by the Session in charity to help him.[287]

But these last scenarios were rare – largely it was old age and the resulting inability to work experienced by so many parishioners that brought them to need help from the Kirk. It is possible that Robert Mearns the elder was on relief for nine years.[288] Ann Criggie, even though she had been the wife of a fairly successful shipmaster and trader, may have had to ask for relief for one year, from 3rd December 1806 to the 29th of November 1807,[289] when she would have been in her seventies. It was perhaps after this that this matriarch of the Gowans died. She had been a monthly "pensioner" of the parish.

Poor relief, then, was varied in its size and means of distribution to the people. It was always a response to poverty, but it seems that there were a whole host of "acceptable" causes of poverty meriting response in the eyes of the Session. This was fortunate for the people of the village, as, for many of them, the Kirk was the only institution to which they could turn for help. Poor relief was the most wide-reaching aspect of welfare on offer from the Kirk, and touched most lives in the village, as poverty was never far away. In this the stories that the fishermen were often very

---

[282] NAS Ref. CH2/34/9-10

[283] NAS Ref. CH2/34/11

[284] NAS Ref. CH2/34/12

[285] NAS Ref. CH2/34/6; Bervie OPRs NAS Ref. RD 254

[286] NAS Ref. CH2/34/1

[287] *Ibid*

[288] NAS Ref. CH2/34/7

[289] *Ibid*

poor is substantiated (if it needed any substantiation;) but we should remember that that was not the whole story – some, like James Gowan, who died in 1800, did leave sizeable amounts of money in their wills.

In terms of education, there was a school established at Bervie from a very early period, maintained by the Kirk and the Burgh Council. Unfortunately no records survive directly relating to the school itself, and all that is known is gleaned from the very vague (and surprisingly lacking in detail) Kirk Session Registers and the Burgh Council Minutes. The Kirk Session and the Council often collaborated on the appointment of the Schoolmaster, and the appointee would often end up on either the Kirk Session, or on the Council, or on both. But, in spite of the lack of information about it, education was, as Devine has put it, *"at the very heart of [the Kirk's] programme for religious revolution,"*[290] and therefore its effects, however poorly documented in Bervie Parish, and in particular in the village of Gourdon, deserve examination.

One interesting note to begin with is that to some extent the people of the village did have some influence on the appointment of the schoolmaster. They had exerted this through their Elders, and, in the early eighteenth century, also through Councillor Robert Dickie, son of Robert Dickie in Gourdon. Councillor Dickie was the first known Gourdon man to reach the dizzy heights of a Bervie Councillor and, as such, was the first man in the village who had the vote.[291]

Even though this was the case, learning to write was not always the priority in a fishing community like Gourdon – usually more people could read, judging from the better statistical information that exists elsewhere in the records of the time. It would appear from the other records of coastal communities in seventeenth century Scotland, such as the journal of Alexander Gillespie of Elie,[292] that some shipmasters as early as this period could read and write. Unfortunately, nothing exists in this period to directly link the Gourdon Masters to the ability to read and write, but it would seem likely that they could. These skills would have been learnt, on payment of a minimal fee, at Bervie School.

It is only with the dawn of the eighteenth century that a significant body of evidence begins to emerge, showing that most of the Gourdon shipmasters were literate, and, in one case, basically numerate. For example, James Gowan, (b. 1706), probably brother of John Gowan who had the Shore Inn, is said to have "regularly corresponded" with his mother. This can only have been done through letters, as they were miles apart, (James at Leith, his mother at Gourdon).[293] So James must have been literate. Whether his mother was also able to write, or whether she dictated the replies, is less certain. There is no evidence to show that education in Gourdon extended to the womenfolk, a sad reminder of a time when the men of the village were able to fund education only for those they thought would need it most in the times they lived in – their sons.

In 1751, the minister, Rev. Dow, had the Session Clerk embark on a short-lived but very detailed system of recording the evidence of witnesses in cases brought before the Session. By this system whether or not a person was able to sign their statement was recorded. Fortunately, there was a major case involving the Gourdon people at this date – that of Christian Blews and Robert Freeman (see the previous

---

[290] T. M. Devine, *The Scottish Nation 1700-2000*, (1999) at 91
[291] Bervie Town Council Minute Book, Volume One
[292] F. Watson, *Scotland's Story* (a BBC television documentary)
[293] R. Gowans, *Op. cit.*

section of this Chapter).[294] Five Gourdon people – three men and two women – gave evidence in this case. Of them, only one of the men could write – Robert Mearns, perhaps nephew of the elder of the same name. The other two men, who were Jeamies, were probably similarly related to shipmasters, but were illiterate. So a family connection of this sort did not guarantee literacy at this time.

Therefore action was finally taken to remedy this situation. In 1773, Rev. Dow put some of the Session's money into the school, to make provision to teach "poor scholars."[295] Whether this initial action had much effect cannot be discerned, but at least Dow had identified the problem and was working on a remedy to solve it.

But education was largely the preserve, for most of this period in Gourdon, of the male shipmasters, the only people who really needed, so it was thought, to be fully literate, to keep records of their voyages, cargoes and details of their crews. Since on occasion they also needed to produce evidence in paper form of where their ship had come from, this requirement would have been even greater. To what extent this education liberated the minds of the fishermen cannot be known – in many ways they were liberated enough as it was!

Healthcare is the least well documented of the aspects of parish welfare at Bervie. However, one does gain brief glimpses of some attempts to improve the health of the villagers.

Throughout most of the history of Gourdon, there was usually some woman in the village who would be almost the "NHS" to the others there, providing a service literally from "cradle to grave." In more recent times, Anne Gowan, (1845-1928), who was the wife of Alexander Moncur and the great-granddaughter of Robert Gowan and Ann Criggie, performed this role (her photograph is on the Dedication page). She was always on hand as the midwife at the birth of a child in the village, and she would have been in attendance when one of the villagers was dying, to look after them in their final days. She is said to have practised herbal medicine, showing that there was some knowledge in the village of natural remedies for ailments.[296]

But, of course, by this time Anne Gowan was working in conjunction with the doctor at Bervie - in the early twentieth century, a Dr. Aymer[297] - and with a growing (but still very expensive) post-Victorian national healthcare system. When the problems of the villagers were beyond her skill, there was the possibility that others might be able to help.

Back in the seventeenth century, there was almost no such help. Anne Gowan's predecessors constituted the sole means of help available for the villagers, and, while their aid definitely saved lives, as did Gowan's own help later on, sometimes a different approach to medicine was required which they were not trained to give. Even so, there were miraculous success stories. In 1732, the first recorded Gourdon midwife, Jean Greig, successfully delivered a child which was two months premature, and who went on to survive.[298] The skill of these women must not be underestimated. For example, it is said that in the case of premature children, one way in which they tried to revive the infants in later times was to give them drops of whisky from a feather. This method was probably in use in the seventeenth and eighteenth centuries as well.

---

[294] NAS Ref. CH2/34/1/175-176
[295] NAS Ref. CH2/34/1
[296] Traditions recalled by Mrs Jessie Smith Christie (nee Moncur) (1904-1982) and Mrs Annie Gowans Pittock (nee Mowat) (1909-2004)
[297] Tradition recalled by Mrs Jessie Smith Christie (nee Moncur) (1904-1982)
[298] NAS Ref. CH2/34/14

Yet, Rev. Dow and the Session saw that sometimes the skill of the women was not enough. So, for the first time, on October 29th 1749, Dow and the Session decided that the collection for that week should be used as a donation for the Infirmary at Aberdeen.[299] Probably he hoped that this donation would encourage those among his parishioners who were ill to go to the hospital, or at least to encourage the hospital to admit patients from Bervie. The collection for the Infirmary was taken every year after this, to 1800 and beyond.

For some reason, however, (probably a mixture of the expense involved and an understandable suspicion of the hospitals of the day), no one in Gourdon took the opportunity for some time. Dow's genuinely well-intentioned scheme did not seem to be working.

Eventually, however, someone did come forward. On April 3rd 1763 William Mearns, who might have been the son of Robert Mearns the elder, petitioned the Session to be recommended by them for admittance to the Aberdeen Infirmary. He was described as a *"young man... who has long suffered under sickness."*[300] Once he had provided security that he would not ask the Session to pay any fees for his care, his petition was granted. Dow finally had had some success.

It was to be another year before the next inhabitant of Gourdon would ask to be admitted to the hospital. This time it was another Mearns – Margaret Mearns, perhaps another relative of Robert Mearns the elder, who had suffered under a *"long illness."*[301] The Session again agreed to help.

But after this, it was to be another eleven years before the Session received another such petition. It also seems rather odd that both of the petitioners in the 1760s were possibly so closely connected to Robert Mearns the elder. There are two possible explanations for this. Either the Mearns family was the only family in the village which could afford the help, or Dow had asked Mearns to put the sick members of his own family forward first for treatment, in the hope of encouraging the other villagers to do the same. Sadly, it didn't really work. Only one other inhabitant of the village went to the Infirmary in Dow's time – John Mowat, son of James Mowat, weaver in Gourdon, (see Chapter Five).[302]

The relationship that the Gourdon people had with the Kirk, then, was a very complicated one. On the one hand, it seems that Thom was wrong when he suggested that the villagers were simply not troubled with religion; and the lack of dissent in the parish was not down to this or some simple conservatism. For in the early stages of the period, the community had shown that it was capable of the most dramatic displays of protest in relation to changes within the church that did not meet with its approval. Supporters of Thom might argue that the "religious" feeling of the early eighteenth century was merely a reaction to an oppressive system; once that system began to decline, there was no need to react against it; and so it is quite correct to say that the villagers did not trouble their heads with religion. But the ability to deliver on the discipline system did not decline fully until Thom's own time, and the commitment to the survival thereof was still strong even then. Moreover, in the decades that followed the end of the eighteenth century, a deep commitment to Christianity emerged amongst many of the villagers, and indeed it still endures amongst many of their descendants today. In some way this must surely have built on what had gone before – and the seed of dissenting movements in the village fell on

---

[299] NAS Ref. CH2/34/1
[300] *Ibid*
[301] *Ibid*
[302] *Ibid*

very fertile ground – I know that I am correct in saying that a large Christian Brethren movement grew up in the Gourdon and Bervie area, for example. It is all too easy to take the other line too, which is unfortunately current in popular folk-lore – that the kirk simply used a discipline system to oppress the people – humiliating them into being good Christians. In this line of thought we should see protests against this system, like those in Gourdon, as constituting a catalyst that forced the church to back-track, and to appease the people with a system of welfare. But the kirk has never operated in this fashion. And Dow still did utilise the discipline system in this period. So what can one say?

The key to understanding these rather confused assertions, I believe, lies in understanding the ministry of Thomas Dow, who has to be seen as one of the most successful of the ministers of Bervie. Let us not forget that the actions of the minister act as signposts to the needs of the community to which he was responding; if we accept this, the Session minutes suddenly become alive as a series of responses which elucidate the characters of the villagers.

The period in question began with protest. That is true. However, these protests, in many ways, can be viewed as having failed to achieve much change. The villagers all returned to church after whatever happened on August 20th 1676; and Arnott was still installed as minister in spite of his rather frosty welcome to the parish in 1714. His parishioners' resentment of the establishment seems to have subsided with time; and the discipline system seems to have been accepted – the fact that it was in decline may have helped in this regard. The protests merely tell us that the villagers were willing to "dissent", for want of a better word, if they felt that this was necessary. This does not tell us that they were proto-humanists rebelling against the church; and this certainly does not tell us that they did not care about religion. When Dow was appointed, significantly, there was no repeat of the 1714 incident. The changed attitude must have resulted from a development of some sort in the time of Arnott. It is difficult to speculate on what this might have been; but Arnott does not appear to have reacted with an authoritarian denunciation of the villagers after his "arrest." It might be ventured that the response of the minister, and his character, helped to calm a rather troubled parish. It is speculative, but in this period, the relationship the villagers had with such a prominent local figure would almost certainly have influenced their own characters. But, as I mentioned above, I think it is Dow's ministry that really allows us to understand the change in attitude. His relationship with the villagers, which of course can only be reconstructed based on the Kirk Session records – a point to be borne in mind, but not fatal to the establishment of a somewhat solid conclusion here – suggests that they neither felt themselves simply to be protesting against an abstract concept of the Kirk, nor that they were simply uninterested in religion. It has been shown that Dow did believe in the discipline system; but he also believed that, at times, it was not necessary to punish the villagers as much as was possible to ensure that standards of Christian conduct were maintained. And this is telling too – it shows that the villagers, if given a little encouragement, were willing to co-operate with the minister. And Dow sought to strengthen this relationship, in the form of what he must have seen as Christian outreach of some sort or another, by setting up the grants for poor scholars, and by attempting to show the villagers that there was a way to obtain better healthcare. All this fits with the character of a minister who went out of his way to help his people when they were faced with real danger in the time of Cumberland. I propose that the key to understanding this period of protest and peace lies in the relationship between the minister and the villagers – not in the relationship between an abstract concept of religion and the villagers. Thom ascribed the lack of dissent amongst the villagers towards the church in this period as being down to lack of interest in religion. I disagree, as there clearly *was* a relationship between the minister and the community in this period, and with religion – and I also maintain this point due to later tradition. I would ascribe the lack of dissent simply to the good relationship, that Dow had so carefully built up, between the minister and the people – that, I presume, Rev. Croll further developed. Protest in the earlier period is then, at least partially, to be ascribed to a poor relationship with men like Rait. This seems to me a far more sensible conclusion than that of Thom. In accepting this conclusion, one does not need to say that there was no religion in the village in this period beyond the relationship between the minister and his parishioners; rather, one merely needs to accept that this was a vital factor in shaping the faith and the characters of the villagers.

CHAPTER FIVE:
GOURDON AND THE LAW

"The people... are by no means addicted to litigation."[303]

In the period stretching from the early seventeenth century until the late eighteenth century the institutions of the law again assist in elucidating the changing character of the people of Gourdon. At the beginning of this period, the law appears to have been utilised primarily to keep order amongst the villagers. There is very little evidence to suggest that the villagers concerned themselves much with civil litigation prior to the 1750s. All of the cases that exist in the early period and that relate to the village concern criminal matters of theft and brawling – and it seems that the Kirk sometimes exercised jurisdiction in these areas too. But by the end of the period, the relationship that the people had with the institutions of the law had developed dramatically. Between 1777 and 1791, members of the Gowan family were involved in litigation at Stonehaven Sheriff Court no fewer than seventeen times[304] (so much for the opening quote of this chapter, above, again taken from Thom!). There are many more cases in the minute books of the court that indicate a considerable increase in litigation in this period as a means of resolving disputes. The obvious question, then, to ask is this – why did the villagers increasingly resort to the courts for remedies to their disputes? Why did their relationship with the courts develop so dramatically in this period? Secondly, it has been shown that the Gourdon people were no strangers to popular protest when they felt threatened by developments in institutions of authority – one can think here, in relation to the Kirk, of the incidents in 1676 and 1714. Is there any evidence to suggest that the villagers' relationship with the courts was similarly coloured by a willingness to protest against perceived oppression? Thirdly, it has been shown that many of the Gourdon families became more involved in trade towards the end of the eighteenth century. Did this perhaps influence the increase in litigation? To answer these questions, first of all the early role of the courts in simply maintaining order will be examined, followed by an introduction to the significance of the growth in litigation in the second half of the eighteenth century. This argument will then be developed through a survey of some of the surviving case-law. In dealing with these questions, it shall be argued that there were various factors that did influence the growth of litigation in the late eighteenth century; but one of these probably does relate to the declining influence of the Kirk as an institution designed to maintain social order through the discipline system. This change came about not so much through the ministry of men like Dow, with the *developed* attitude to discipline that he had (as noted above,) but simply through practical considerations – for the villagers, the world no longer stopped at the parish boundary. Economic relationships came to matter increasingly to the villagers; and the Kirk had little authority to regulate these.

As stated, in the early period, it would appear that the primary role of the courts was the maintenance of order. For the purposes of this work only selections from the records of the Sheriff Court at Stonehaven and the Burgh Court at Montrose have been examined. (Trawling through the un-extracted processes for the Court of

---

[303] W. Thom, *Parish of Inverbervie or Bervie*, in Sir John Sinclair (ed.) *Old Statistical Account of Scotland*, Volume XIV – Kincardineshire and South and West Aberdeenshire (1982 reprint) 136-147 at 146
[304] NAS Ref. SC5/4/4

Session and the High Court of Justiciary in this period is not an appealing prospect!) There was a Barony Court at Hallgreen, but very few of the records of this court survive.[305] This may in part be because the records were not themselves kept in individual ledgers; one of the few other records of a process before this court is to be found simply listed in the family papers of Rait of Hallgreen. This record must have constituted some form of evidence before the Barony Court. It consists of an extract from the minutes of the Kirk Session, possibly of Benholm, concerning the case of Arthur Massie, dated 16th February 1668.[306] He was charged with murdering his wife, and, when asked how she had died, he replied that she must have been carried off by a whirlwind! It is not known what the court made of this, unfortunately – but the case was referred up to the Barony Court from the Kirk Session. Some Barony Courts did possess the jurisdiction to try those accused of murder in this period.[307] I am uncertain as to what the position was in relation to the Barony Court of Hallgreen

The earliest case that is recorded concerning the Gourdon fishermen is that found by Robert Gove – the case of Andrew Mearns and David Todd, who were prosecuted for cutting off the tails of the horses owned by the Lairds of Hallgreen, Brunton and Newton, in 1618. Probably they wanted these to make tippens (components in making fishing gear) but whatever the reason for this act, the court was not amused. The fishermen were banished from Kincardineshire for life.[308]

The records of the Sheriff Court are the most useful in relation to elucidating the history of the village. The earliest records for Stonehaven Sheriff Court date from 1650.[309] In July 1654, Robert Allan in Johnshaven gave in a complaint on behalf of John Anderson, who may also have been a Johnshaven fisher, accusing Thomas Fatt in Gourdon and David Fatt in Johnshaven of *"hurting John Anderson and breaking his head with a dirk."*[310] Apparently David Fatt had also *"struck him [Anderson] down in the boat"* and Thomas Fatt had *"struck him in the head with a dirk."* The parties were ordered to appear before the Sheriff Court in Stonehaven on July 21st. At that time the court was held in the old tolbooth, near the harbour in Stonehaven, which is still standing today. Much to the Sheriff's annoyance, only Robert Allan turned up. In their absence the court found the Fatts guilty of the crime in question and fined them fifty merks each for the attack and twenty merks each for failing to turn up in court. Altogether the Fatts were fined one hundred and forty merks Scots – a very large sum of money for an ordinary person to pay in 1654.

These are the only known cases that involved the people of Gourdon that came before the courts of law in the seventeenth century. While I have not trawled through all of the records of processes in civil matters for the latter part of the seventeenth century, of the several boxes I did look through I could find no evidence that the inhabitants of the village were ever involved in such activities. The same is to be said for my researches in the early eighteenth century. There are literally thousands of processes from this period, which are only catalogued in the minute books of the Sheriff Court, and I would not want to pretend that I have looked through them all(!) But I did examine several boxes at random in the earlier period, before the minute

---

[305] NAS Ref. RH11/35/1. Records survive from sittings of the court on 6th January 1673 and 4th August 1673 only.

[306] *Arthur Massie* (1668) NAS Ref. RH15/37/119

[307] See W. Croft Dickinson, *The Court Book of the Barony of Carnwarth 1523-1542* (1938) xxvi-xxvii; xxxix-xliv

[308] *Andrew Mearns and David Todd* (1618) as cited in R. Gove, *Gourdon in the Nineteenth Century*

[309] NAS Ref. SC5/1/1

[310] *PF Stonehaven v Fatt and Fatt* (1654) NAS Ref. SC5/1/2

books were in use, and could find no references to civil litigation in the village. It seems to me that the main contact with the law that the villagers had related to the maintenance of order – that is to say, the prevention of crime. Naturally this could be disproved, but I feel that this is unlikely. In the earlier period, the Kirk Session still dealt with most disputes – for example, one can think here of the case, in 1656, of Thomas and John Mearns, who were rebuked for fighting in public.[311] In 1732, in the case involving Agnes Gowan, it does not appear to have occurred to the aggrieved parties to take the case up to the Sheriff Court. Moreover, if it is correct to argue, as was attempted above, that the victims of the verbal attack in that case were not satisfied with the decision of the Session, then the remedy countenanced appears to again have involved an appeal to the local authority of the Kirk. There are two possible reasons for this. The first is that the people were unable to afford legal representation in the courts. I find this unlikely, as the villagers were never *that* poor, especially if one gives any credence to the tradition that one of their number left three sloops to his sons on his death. The second option seems the more sensible to me. The villagers were happy with the justice of the Kirk Session in this period and still defined the component of their relationships that focussed on the maintenance of equity within the community with reference to the church's authority. Perhaps this was supplemented by the justice of the Hallgreen Barony Court, but the role of that court in the early eighteenth century is unclear– the only references to the court that I have found concern seventeenth century disputes. *Prima facie*, the position in relation to the role of the justice of the Session was reversed in the later case of *Walker and Jeamie v Milne and Allan* (1778),[312] a case again concerning defamatory remarks that this time went to the Sheriff Court, with no reference to the Kirk Session. But, as shall be shown in due course, the change was not as dramatic as one might think.

The majority of cases in this period concerned debts owed by one party to another. There is one early case, dated 1733, in the records of Montrose Burgh Court, concerning one Margaret Gowans in Montrose – it is possible that she may have been connected to the Gowan family – if so, this is the first known civil process concerning an individual from the village.[313] Margaret was involved in a dispute with a Montrose writer (solicitor) called Alexander Jamieson, who had persistently refused to pay her her due salary for having worked as the servant of David Wyse, first in Mains of Lauriston, then in Montrose. This consisted of five pounds Scots, an ell of cloth and an apron. In the end the case went before the Montrose Bailie, John Doers. At first Jamieson insisted that the whole fee had been paid, but then changed his mind half way through the case, saying *"at least some of it"* had been paid. Gowans did not change her story. Perhaps because of this, Doers found in her favour, and awarded her her legal costs. The case is, however, very early; and even if Gowans had been from Gourdon originally, it tells us little about the prevailing attitudes of the villagers at this time – Gowans herself must have been away from Gourdon for years.

The first civil process that I have found concerning the people of Gourdon is the case of *Law and Watt v Jamie and Mearns*.[314] This case again concerned debts, this time owed to Robert Law, fisher in Gourdon, and his wife Jean Watt, by

[311] NAS Ref. CH2/34/10

[312] *Walker and Jeamie v Milne and Allan* (1778) NAS Ref. SC5/8/93

[313] *Gowans v Wyse's Executor* (1733) M/P/15/148/7

[314] *Law and Watt v Jamie and Mearns* (1753) NAS Ref. SC5/8/50. Recent research shows that there was, actually, one (but only one) known earlier process recorded in the minute books on 3rd July 1745 – *John Crombie in Johnshaven v John Mearns in Gourdon*. There were five cases from Gourdon heard in the 1750s, all involving pursuers from Gourdon. See NAS Ref. SC5/4/1-6.

Alexander Jamie, fisher in Gourdon and Robert Mearns, fisher in Gourdon – who may also have been the same person as Robert Mearns the Kirk Elder mentioned in Chapter Four. Mearns's debt was three pounds Scots, which was the money due to Jean Watt for having worked for him as his servant for half a year. (It is interesting to note that most Gourdon shipmasters of this period had at least one, sometimes two, servants.) Jamie's debts had been accumulated over a much longer period of time – including cash lent to him to buy mussels the year he was married and cash lent by Jean Watt to him to lay his boat's keel when it was blown out of the harbour. The court found against Jamie and Mearns. It is interesting to note that this case concerned the economic relationships between the villagers – relationships that the Kirk traditionally did not control to any great extent, in this parish at least. It cannot be said that the villagers had never lent each other cash before – surely they had – but now these economic relationships were becoming significant enough to cause the villagers to seek means to ensure that they were respected. If the Kirk would not provide this, or could not provide this, the institutions of the law would.

In terms of legal representation, usually a Stonehaven or Montrose writer would be chosen by the villagers to ensure the success of their actions. Colin Alison of Montrose was frequently used, as were George Milne and John Milne from Stonehaven, in the latter eighteenth century. James Strachan, the smuggler mentioned in Chapter Three above, also appears frequently in the records as the Montrose messenger of the Burgh Court. The lawyers did refer to legal authorities, *Erskine* in particular,[315] and *Bankton*.[316]

Good legal representation mattered. In 1772, James Watt, fisher in Gourdon, became indebted to John Jamie, shipmaster in Gourdon, after purchasing goods from him worth £0/2/11.[317] Jamie took Watt to court to get his money, and, when the tax on the goods was added to the debt, along with the legal costs of the case, the total amount claimed by Jamie consisted of £1/9/11 sterling. When Watt still failed to make payment, a letter of horning was issued against him on April 21st, declaring him to be a *"rebel"* and necessitating his imprisonment. On May 19th, James Strachan, along with John Fraser, indweller in Montrose, and Robert Walsh from Falside, marched down the Gourdon brae to arrest Watt and to carry him off to prison in the Montrose Tolbooth. He was to be kept there *"in closs prison and confinement, aye, and while he make compleat payment satisfaction to John Jamie the Complainer."* This would have been difficult, as Watt had literally nothing – he could not pay Jamie anything back. And so, as he sat in the dark of the tollbooth, Watt must rather have thought that the situation was beyond repair. So it would have been, if he had not had a friend in Gourdon.

The role of James Mowat, the Gourdon weaver who hailed from Kineff and Catterline, is not entirely clear in this case. He was described at one point as Watt's *"procurator"* which infers he was his legal representative. This is not strictly accurate as Colin Alison was the lawyer who dealt with the case on Watt's behalf. It seems feasible that Mowat, in fact, represented Watt in a slightly different way. Mowat himself probably arrived in Gourdon in about 1760, from Fernyflett farm in Kinneff and Catterline Parish. The local community, through the Kirk Session, had been very supportive of his family during the financially difficult period the Mowats faced after James's wife gave birth to twins. Perhaps Watt had shown him friendship at this time. We really don't know. What, then, can we make of Mowat's role as

---

[315] See, for example, the later case of *Crab v Gowans* (1807) NAS Ref. SC5/8/200
[316] *Ibid*
[317] *Jamie v Watt* (1772) M/P/15/148/7

Watt's *"procurator"*? The answer may be quite simple. Watt had no means of securing his release from prison. He had no money, and it would not seem likely that a lawyer, out of the goodness of his heart, would go round the tolbooth prisoners to research their cases to see if they could be released. It seems more likely to me that Mowat "represented" Watt by going to Alison in Montrose, agreeing to pay Watt's legal fees if the case went against him. This is not clear from the records; but it is a very plausible explanation of the situation described.

On May 21st, Alison drafted a petition, for the attention of the Magistrates of Montrose, containing, on behalf of Watt, the poignant statement:

"I your prisoner am so poor that I cannot aliment myself in prison."

This was not, however, an appeal to the better nature of the Montrose Magistrates, but a rather strong legal case. Apparently, according to the *"thirty-second Act of the Sixth Session of King William's Parliament,"* if a prisoner could not aliment himself in these circumstances, that is to say provide basic nourishment and clothing to keep himself in some standard of living while in prison, then the pursuer would either have to pay three shillings whenever, in the eyes of the court, Watt had need of it, to pay for his upkeep, or else the pursuer would have to agree to the prisoner's release.

The Montrose Baillie, John Livie, was then presented with this petition. He seems to have taken pity on the impoverished fisherman, and accepted the petition. Allison, and Mowat wasted no time in acting on this. Having gathered all of the by now lengthy papers pertinent to the case they made for Gourdon, to present Jamie with the ultimatum. One can imagine the "speak" in the village as the lawyer and the weaver arrived, case notes in Mowat's hand, marching down the road, to John Jamie's house. Mowat knocked on the door. As always in the community, by now all those watching eyes would have been taking sides in the dispute.

The door was duly answered, but not by Jamie – by his wife, who announced that her husband was not at home. Undeterred, Mowat and Allison, along with two witnesses, John Duncan and Robert Scott, servants to James Grieg, "Vinter in Gourdon," went in, and Mowat read to her the ultimatum, and then wrote out a copy of the papers relating to the case, leaving them in her keeping to show Jamie when he returned. The law thus satisfied they left, and Jamie now had ten days to act. When he returned he must have realised that he was beaten. One instalment of the aliment would amount to more than the original debt!

On June 4th, Colin Allison went again to the Baillie. He was relieved to discover that no aliment had been paid, and so *"creaved that the poor prisoner might be sett at Liberty."* The same day victory was at hand, when the Baillie declared that there should be given *"warrant to the Town Officer to Liberate the said James Watt from the Tolbooth of this Burgh."*

What makes this case of particular interest is the role of Mowat in it. We will probably never know what motivated Mowat to support Watt, but it does not seem unreasonable to suggest that he had agreed to pay Watt's legal fees if the case had not been successful. The community did still matter – it would be wrong to say that the growing importance of economic relationships between the villagers in itself *undermined* the community in this period – but it did provide a new context within which these relationships existed.

There is an interesting postscript to this story. Twenty-two years later, the tables were turned on John Jamie, when James Barry, a Stonehaven butcher, sued the former Gourdon Shipmaster, by then in Montrose, for a debt of £2/13/2. This time no one in Gourdon spoke up for the debtor. He was ordered by the Court to pay the debt back in full and Barry's legal fees.[318]

Having begun with this initial survey of some of the more interesting cases in this period, it is now important to turn to the key question – why was there such a dramatic increase in litigation at this time? I have suggested throughout this section that economic relationships were becoming rapidly more important to the villagers; and the kirk had very little ability, within the system of discipline, to ensure that these relationships were respected; and so the villagers found it necessary to turn to the institutions of the law to ensure that debts were paid. But why this change? Why were economic relationships becoming more important? In the case of one of the Gowans, the answer was obvious – as was shown in Chapter Three above, their trading ventures necessitated the existence of contracts. The contract for the sale of James Gowan's sloop has already been noted.[319] But the commercial relationships involved, as can be seen from a few of the seventeen cases mentioned above from 1777 to 1791, were becoming increasingly more complicated. In *Grant, Factor for Lord Elgin, v Alexander Gowan, Shipmaster in Gourdon*[320] the case centred on the use of bills of exchange, (a bill of exchange being a negotiable instrument akin to a cheque). The same was the case in *Alexander Bruce v Ann Criggie (Mrs Gowan) and Robert Gowan her husband.*[321] This was a remarkably complicated case which involved the question of whether or not a bill of exchange had been transferred to Ann Criggie and her husband Robert Gowan from their son John Gowan by virtue of a factory[322] executed by the said John Gowan in favour of his father, prior to his going on a trading voyage abroad! (If this had been the case, on the facts here, a debt owed by Ann Criggie to Alexander Bruce, upon whom the bill had been drawn, would have been partially cancelled out.) If this were not complicated enough already, the parties then proceeded to squabble, for want of a better word, over the evidence for months, Ann Criggie continuing to remember fresh evidence that helped her case(!). Furthermore, in *Smith v Gowans*[323] one can see the sort of commercial relationship that gave rise to these complexities. In this case, Alexander Gowan, master of the *Isobel* of Gourdon, entered into a contract with Alexander Smith in Burn of Maurdie to deliver two cargoes of lime shells to the harbour at Little Johnshaven at a time of his choosing between 1st April and 1st June 1787 – and the contract included a term in restraint of trade – during this period he was not to ship goods for any other parties. He was to be paid two shillings sterling – half on delivery and the other half on 1st February 1788. To improve the tenor of the agreement, Gowan agreed to ship some of the shells from Sunderland. If either party failed in carrying out his side of the bargain a £10 penalty would be due to be paid by the defaulting party to the innocent party. One can see that the Kirk, the traditional means of regulating most relationships in Gourdon, did not carry the legal apparatus to deal with such matters. It has already been suggested that the reason that the Gowans, and other families like them, turned to trade away from fishing may have been that the fishing was in trouble in this period.

---

[318] *Barry v Jamie* (1794) M/P/15/108/1
[319] *Alexander v Gowans* (1790) NAS Ref. SC5/8/135
[320] *Grant v Gowans* (1787) NAS Ref. SC5/8/115
[321] *Bruce v Criggie or Gowan and Gowan* (1787) NAS Ref. SC5/8/116
[322] A document conferring power on Robert Gowan to manage his son's business affairs.
[323] *Smith v Gowans* (1787) NAS Ref. SC5/8/116

The growing importance of commerce to the villagers does not, however, explain many of the cases in this period. Why were there so many cases pertaining to small debts? The dates of some of the cases speak for themselves here. For example, in the late 1770s, there was an action brought at the instance of James Wilson, a shipmaster in either Johnshaven or Stonehaven, against David Lownie, whitefisher in Gourdon (and ancestor of the later Lownies of Gourdon). The debt due was £0/9/3.[324] There were at least seven other cases involving Gourdon litigants in the 1770s.[325] Perhaps part of the reason behind this large amount of litigation related to the fact that there was some considerable hardship in this period. This is illustrated in connection with the story of the Meal Mob Riots (see below) that took place in 1778. Hardship, then, also resulted in certain individuals being unable to pay off debts.

So, why did people not turn to the law to settle their disputes before the late eighteenth century? There had always been hardship; and I am sure that there had always been debts. It is true the more complex legal relationships necessitated by the greater trade from the village only appear to been required in the latter eighteenth century, reflecting commercial reality; but this in itself will not suffice to explain the dearth of legal material before the 1750s.

One case sheds particular light on this point – the case of *Walker and Jeamie v Milne and Allan.*[326] I mentioned this case earlier on in this chapter, as bearing significant parallels to the case of Agnes Gowan (heard before the Kirk Session) in 1732. On January 28th 1778, Margaret Jeamie, wife of Robert Walker, Skipper in Gourdon, brought a case before the Sheriff Court at Stonehaven, along with her husband, against Janet Allan, wife of James Milne, Mariner in Gourdon. Apparently, Janet and her husband *"in presence of a great number of people at sundry different times,"* had called Jeamie a *"whore, a thief and a murderer."* One can observe at the outset a great similarity to the case of Agnes Gowan. Therefore, Jeamie wanted to sue Janet Allan and her husband, claiming damages of fifty pounds sterling (a vast sum of money – in 1800, one of the wealthiest Gourdon fishers of this period, had life savings amounting to that sum).[327] She also wanted:

> *"the said Janet Allan... to be decerned...to appear at the...*
> **Kirk of Bervie**, *bare-headed and bare-footed* **on an Sunday at**
> **disolving the congregation** *from* **Divine Service**, *and there on her knees,*
> *audibly confess her fault...and ask* **pardon**, **first of God**, *then of the*
> *Complainer...and say, false tongue, thou lied in uttering the*
> *above injurious expressions."* [Emphasis added.]

So clearly Jeamie did not want Allan to get off lightly! But I think that there is more to be said in relation to this statement – and this, I think, allows us to see that a reading that simply views litigation as a replacement for the Kirk in regulating relationships in Gourdon in this period as wholly inadequate. The remedy that Jeamie sought, perhaps suggesting that she may have been one of the *"unco' guid,"* proves something far more significant about the character of the people. First of all, let us remember what has been demonstrated so far. In this period, the discipline system was used by Thomas Dow as part of his attempt to stimulate a better relationship between the minister and the people, and *in so doing* to encourage Christian behaviour

---

[324] *Wilson v Lownie* (1777) NAS Ref. SC5/8/92
[325] NAS Ref. SC5/4/4
[326] *Walker and Jeamie v Milne and Allan* (1778) NAS Ref. SC5/8/3
[327] NAS Ref. CC20/4/28

amongst his flock. The role of the Kirk in the community was being very subtly redefined. Secondly, economic relationships were becoming more important to the villagers. Litigation was, therefore, increasing in importance, as a result of commercial enterprise and due to the villagers' growing awareness that the courts were useful in securing the return of debts. Thirdly, as shown in the Mowat incident, economic relationships were not all that mattered to the villagers in this period. There is a fourth point to note here that is of some import. It was recently pointed out to me by Professor Forte of Aberdeen University that the above quotation may, in fact, have been taken from a style akin to that in the Aberdeen Stylebook of 1722. He suggests in his article on the subject that *"The probable reason of compelling this self-denunciation, and requiring the transgressor to add that he knew of nothing to indicate that the victim was anything other than "ane honest man" was to restore to the latter his reputation: an important commodity in a relatively close-knit society."*[328] Hence it may be unfair to label Jeamie as being one of the *"unco' guid."* Her reasoning for seeking the denunciatory authority of the Kirk is thus not entirely clear. Nonetheless, whether she sought simple revenge or whether she wanted the restoration of her good reputation (or both, which seems plausible) what is of interest is the way in which she went about achieving either or both of these ends.

A simplistic juxtaposition of the case of Jeamie in 1778 and Gowans in 1732 might result in the conclusion that the courts had, in the eyes of the villagers, become the new forum for the resolution of disputes. The Kirk Session's will to execute discipline in all circumstances was declining; perhaps this explains the villagers' interest in the law. But this is not anywhere near the whole picture. I mentioned in the last chapter that I feel that Thom was grossly mistaken to argue that the people of Gourdon did not trouble their heads with religion, as he put it, in this period, and again, I think, from their actual attitude to the courts themselves we can see that he was wrong. Jeamie wanted a financial remedy; but she also wanted something else. She wanted both the old discipline system and the court system which the villagers were now more readily prepared to access in order to punish Allan as harshly as possible. Note the highlighted words in the quote above. The courts may have been looked to to enforce the discipline – perhaps reinforcing the argument I made earlier that Dow himself had indeed subtly developed the application of the system in the parish – but, nonetheless, it was discipline that Jeamie wanted. She wanted Allan to be publicly humiliated in the very precinct of the Kirk – immediately after *"Divine Service."* The Kirk really mattered to the people. It was still very much at the heart of the community. If a person wanted the moral authority to say that his or her neighbour was at fault – slapping the splinter out of his or her eye – or to restore his or her reputation, as per the point made by Professor Forte, then still the villagers thought that the place to do this was the Kirk. Only the church had the moral authority to see that act done – to somehow validate it. Note how the pardon to be asked of the pursuer is equated with the pardon to be asked of God. The reference to the bare head and the bare feet carry overtones of sackcloth and ashes. On the point made in Chapter Four, anyone who doubts the significance of religion in the village in this period should now be satisfied that such concerns are groundless. Yet I do not wish to make the mistake either of viewing this as a characteristic of the people of Gourdon alone. This sort of thinking was, perhaps, commonplace across Scotland.

---

[328] A. D. M. Forte and M. C. Meston, *Legal Life in Aberdeen in the Early Nineteenth Century – The Aberdeen Stylebook of 1722* in the *Aberdeen University Review*, LIX, no. 207, Spring 2002 p. 197-208 at 204-205. I am grateful to Professor Forte for this reference. Any errors, however, in interpreting the particular references in this case remain my own.

This story of the villagers is symptomatic of the way in which many in the localities sought the resolution of disputes throughout the eighteenth century. One must remember the parallel between the quotation regarding Allan's penance and that found in the Aberdeen Stylebook. Furthermore, the legal writer Erskine, in his *An Institute of the Law of Scotland*,[329] notes that in cases of verbal injury, *"If the offender be poor, the commissaries usually ordain him to do penance, by making a public recantation in the church, or in the church door. And sometimes these two penalties of fine and penance are conjoined."* In Gourdon, therefore, as in other communities in this period, the role of the Kirk was clearly still vitally important.

The increase in litigation, then, does not tell us that the villagers had all read some simplified form of Adam Smith, re-orientated their lives around economic relationships to ensure that they could be regulated by the authority of the law, in the face of a weakening Kirk, and that they then abandoned the concept of bonds through Kirk and community in exchange for bonds given in the hope of getting money. The increase in litigation was in itself a result of economic changes in the life of the village necessitating greater trade, coupled with a subtly redefined role for the Session. This is the proper reading of the situation. The role of the Kirk in the community did not *decline*; it *developed* – until the beginning of the nineteenth century, at any rate. The villagers still viewed the essential bond that drew the community together as lying in the church. This point truly sheds light on the lives and characters of the villagers. They had grasped the significance of the courts in their lives; but the decline in instances of the exercise of discipline does not indicate a decline in the importance of the Kirk to the people.

After the writing of this rather revealing tract, Janet Allan was summoned by James Strachan, on January 29th, to appear before the Sheriff Depute on February 5th in connection with the matter. But she was not one to take this lying down, and at least her husband had a fairly good alibi. She told this to her lawyer, John Duncan, who drafted a defence for his client, which was presented to what must have become an astonished court on February 5th.

Duncan began by pointing out that Milne could not be liable. The poor man knew nothing of any of this – he had been taken by the press-gang six months before, and was over three thousand miles away!

The lawyer then went on to suggest legal reasons for why "the process ought to be dismist." Firstly, he argued that the case was a criminal nature, and so it needed the support of the Procurator Fiscal to continue – it had not had this support. The modern lawyer might view this as somewhat bizarre. Every first year law student hopefully knows that defamation is a civil and not a criminal matter. But in the eighteenth century things were somewhat different. Erskine treats defamation under crimes.[330] The legal writer Hume, writing a few decades later, noted that an offence of falsely accusing a person of a criminal act had been recognised by the courts, being *"a far more serious and prejudicial slander than the using of reproachful, but loose and passionate appellations, such as thief, adulterer and the like...."* The recognition of this crime in the earlier period is noted by the seventeenth century writer MacKenzie.[331] But even in this early period MacKenzie notes that *"The Criminal*

---

[329] Erskine, *Institute*, (1773) IV, 4, 81

[330] Erskine, *Institute* (1773) IV, 4, 80-81

[331] MacKenzie, *The Laws and Customs of Scotland In Matters Criminal*, (2005 reprint of the 1678 original, with an introduction by J. Chalmers, C. Gane and F. Leverick of Aberdeen University), I, XXX. I am grateful to Mr. Chalmers for bringing this reference to my attention; any errors, however, in interpreting the material in question remain my own.

Courts likewise punishes verbal injuries, if against Magistrats, but will not sustain a pursuite against privat persons...." Hume was of the view that such issues were *"fitter subjects of process in the civil court."* Yet clearly the point was arguable, and clearly Duncan had done his homework on the matter. Secondly, he argued that it was more customary for Commissary Courts, rather than Sheriff Courts, to deal with *"verball injuries,"* and so Duncan questioned the jurisdiction of the Sheriff Depute in this matter. Again, this argument was well founded in law.[332] Thirdly, since her husband could not be cited, Duncan stated that the law showed that any sentence against Allan could not be carried out *"till after the disolution of her present marriage."* Again this defence, while perhaps seeming bizarre to us, was actually well founded in law, as the husband was regarded as curator to his wife, and so Erskine noted that *"no suit [could] proceed against the wife till [her husband] be cited as defender for his interest."*[333]

The final defence was more startling. Janet Allan recounted what had sparked the argument in the first place – comments, she said, which were made by Jeamie:-

> *"That she [Allan] was a damned returnal Limmer and ought to be taken to the head of a Hill and burnt to death into dust."*

It always strikes me that eighteenth century people were much more inventive with their insults than we are today! After adding *"several other injurious words"* and *"scandalous epithets,"* Jeamie had then gone to tear *"all her [Allan's] head cloathes to pieces,"* and then she *"beat, bruised and struck her to the great effusion of her blood and imminent danger of her life."* Janet Allan stated that this worked her up into a *"passion,"* and that, basically, she could not remember (and was not responsible for) her actions thereafter! Jeamie had been, apparently, *"the first transgressor,"* and so was *"equally guilty."* Unfortunately it is not clear what the courts made of these rather confused statements of law and fact; we only have part of the court process – the final interlocutor in the case has not survived. However, I did not note any reference in the Kirk Session minutes as to any denunciation of Allan.

There is one final case, from 1778, that sheds some further light on the character of the people of the village. This infers that, while the villagers had not recently targeted the Kirk as the subject of their propensity to popular protest, they had lost none of their zeal for such activity when the situation required it. In late 1778, meal, one of the staples of the Scottish diet, was very scarce in Bervie – in fact in many places throughout the country. This delighted most of the lairds and merchants, who saw a real opportunity to sell off what meal there was at inflated prices.

According to tradition, the Viscount of Arbuthnott was no exception. If the story concerning his actions is to be accepted, one evening, at Arbuthnott House, he was dining with his family, when the subject arose as to what was to be done with the meal there was. He decided to sell what meal there was "to the dogs" (i.e. the black market). The intermediary merchant was to be Robert Napier, Burgess of Bervie, and a notorious smuggler (see Chapter Three Section Two).

However, the Viscount was somewhat indiscreet in making his plans thus. One of his servants, Janet Alexander, from Gourdon, overheard the whole discussion. She resolved to return to the village to inform the people there, where the want was so

---

[332] This is seen from Erskine, *Institute*, I, 5, 30; however the discussion there shows that jurisdiction in this matter was developing in this period.
[333] Erskine, *Institute*, I, 6, 21

great, of the plans. It was clear by this stage that the poorer people would go hungry if no action was taken to stop the sale of the meal on the black market. Worse, it transpired that the food was not even to be re-sold locally, but transported further afield to get better prices. When this became clear, she knew something had to be done.[334]

The evening she returned, the Gourdon people gathered together to hear what she had to say. One can imagine the local outrage when they heard the news, and it spread quickly, soon reaching Bervie and Johnshaven. Especially angry were the women of the parish, who at once decided that, whatever else, the meal must not leave Bervie.

Meanwhile, Arbuthnott had already sold on the subject of all this furore – the meal itself – to Napier, and several of the people in Bervie tried to procure some from him – John Norrie and James Stephen, weavers in Bervie and Robert Dickie, a wright there, being among them – but to no avail. The mood of the people began to blacken, and several of the Gourdon women, led by Margaret Criggie, wife of James Gowan in Gourdon (probably b. 1739, son of John Gowan who had the Shore Inn), marched along the Low Road and confronted Napier in the Square at Bervie. They demanded that he should hand over some meal, because, as Margaret Criggie put it, she had *"four children, besides her husband and herself, and the scarcity was so great she was obliged to buy potatoes for their support."* As the scene turned ugly, Napier evaded the mob again, and decided that he had to act quickly. He sent a message to Alexander Law, Shipmaster in Johnshaven, asking him to come with haste in his sloop to take the meal to Borrowstoness, where it would be sold on. Napier then tried to get carters prepared to carry the meal to the shore.[335]

However, although the sloop arrived on the Saturday of the week in question, there seems to have been some sort of delay in delivery. Somehow word got out about the planned transport via Law's sloop, and doubtless the next day the whole community, at Bervie Kirk, would have been giving dirty looks to Napier, as he tried to pay attention to Rev. Dow's sermon, uncomfortably squirming in the knowledge that he was the most hated man in the parish.

But the people did more than glare. They had laid their plans, seven of the instigators thereof being Janet Allan and Margaret Jamie (bitter enemies seven months before, now by desperate want made allies), Mary Jamie, Jean Allan, Martha Colvin, Christian Blews and Ann Criggie from Gourdon. Christian Blews was the wife of Alexander Gowan, and Ann Criggie the wife of Andrew Mearns.

As Napier came down the brae the next day, heading towards the sloop while escorting his meal, he must have been hoping for a quiet escape. However, he was in for a very nasty shock. After running the gauntlet through the Bervie streets, pelted with stones, he arrived at the shore only to find that the Gourdon women had taken Law prisoner and seized the boat. As upwards of twenty rioters moved towards him, all baying for his blood, and his meal, his nerve broke and he and the carters fled back to Bervie, abandoning the much fought over meal to the mob. The caskets were forced open and the food, at last, was distributed to the people. While it was being handed out Law was kept prisoner, and the Gourdon women held him captive until the next day when they ordered him to leave. He was glad to do so because, as he put it, he *"would have done anything to have been in safety."* The immediate need for

---

[334] R. Gowans, *Op. cit.*
[335] J. Andersen, *The Black Book of Kincardineshire*, (1879) at 81-83

meal satisfied, the mob dispersed, and the Gourdon women quickly made their way back to their homes.

Napier, of course, was infuriated. He at once went to Stonehaven, where he ensured that criminal proceedings were brought against the twenty-one ring-leaders of the rioters. The seven Gourdon women were likewise summoned, and arrived, presumably by sea, at Stonehaven, soon after. There could be only one verdict against them. Jean Allan was imprisoned for three months and then banished from Kincardineshire; Mary Jamie and Janet Allan were imprisoned for two months; Ann Criggie, Ann Taylor, Martha Colvin and Christian Blews were given fourteen days in the jougs; and Margaret Jamie, who got off very lightly, was imprisoned only until she could find caution (security) for her good behaviour for two years, which was also a condition levied on the others on trial. If they broke the law again, they would have to pay a fine of three hundred merks – a huge sum of money. Central authority wanted to make it very clear that such behaviour would not be tolerated.

However, the Gourdon people refused to accept the judgement of the Court. Although not supported in the records, tradition has it that the Gourdon men did not leave their womenfolk in the jougs for long. They were being held in a room with a thatched roof in Stonehaven. Fourteen days after they were imprisoned, it is said, the women were stealthily rescued by their relatives who, having slipped past the guards, lifted the prisoners out of the cell through a hole they had cut in the roof. After that it was a frantic scramble down to the harbour, and then away, by boat, to the safety of Gourdon. If the story is true, the Court did not pursue them. And there is cause to believe it. As Whatley has written:-

> *"attempts on the part of the authorities to take prisoners*
> *were resisted, interpreted as actions which had no legitimacy…*
> *efforts were made… to release anyone who was arrested or imprisoned."*[336]

The relationship between the villagers and the legal institutions, then, gives us further insight into the nature of the community at the end of the eighteenth century. It was a changing community, which did require legal structures to regulate the economic ties that were built up between the villagers and their trading partners. But it was also a very conservative community – it was not simply the economic relationships amongst the villagers that mattered. The processes of the courts, then, coupled with the other evidence that has been put together concerning the history of the village, provide what must be seen as key evidence – particularly in the case of Jeamie and Allan in 1778 – about the key focal points around which the community identified itself. And, once again, the law gives us what must be one of the greatest stories concerning the Gourdon community – the story of the popular protests at the time of the Meal Mob Riots. In particular, if the story that the womenfolk were released by the men of the village from prison after sentence is true, the story of Gourdon can truly be seen in the context of some of the larger social movements of the time. It is now important to turn to the conclusions that can be drawn in relation to the character of the villagers in this period.

---

[336] C. Whatley, *Scottish Society 1707-1830*, (2000) at 174

CONCLUSION

In 1800, the village of Gourdon had already stood for at least five hundred years. In that time it had grown into a small yet significant fishing and trading centre. The pattern of growth continued into the nineteenth century and a new harbour, designed by Thomas Telford, was built to serve the village in 1819. It was in this period that many new families came to the village, and they left the mark of their characters and traditions upon it as much as the fishermen of Yorkshire who first arrived in the village centuries before. The Mowats had already arrived in the village in the late eighteenth century, as had the Lownies (by tradition the "patriarch" of the family was from Ireland); they were later joined by other well-known Gourdon families, like the Craigs (descended from Joseph Craig from Portlethen and Margaret Gowan, one of the Gourdon family) and the Moncurs (descended from James Moncur from Crawton and his wife Elizabeth Christie). The stories of their lives and characters could easily fill another book, much larger than this; and stories concerning their characters are not yet forgotten. The religious revival of the 1860s, for example, contributed greatly to the story of the village; and in this period too was built the first chapel in Gourdon – the Mission Hall. Many of the people of Gourdon later left the village and went even as far afield as Europe and America, like David Douglas Gowan, grandson of Alexander Gowan and Helen Kemlo, who was the first European to discover the Tonto Natural Bridge in Arizona, after a run-in with Apache Indians.

But the aim of this work has always been to seek to uncover something of the nature of the community of Gourdon in the earlier period, in particular in the late seventeenth and eighteenth centuries. At the outset this may have seemed a rather difficult task; many people are under the mistaken impression that very few records survive pertaining to such communities. As has been shown, the truth is rather different, at least from the mid-seventeenth century onwards.

Up to now, there have been only two testaments as to the character of the villagers in this period. The first consisted of oral traditions; and the second was the Old Statistical Account for Inverbervie, written in the 1790s by Mr. Walter Thom, manufacturer in Bervie, and later Captain of the local "home guard," as it were, in the Napoleonic era. He stated that the villagers *"neither plagued their heads with politics nor religion,"* and that they *"were by no means addicted to litigation."* In relation to politics the picture remains unclear. But it is clear that Christianity played a central role in the shaping of the characters of the villagers in this period; and it is also clear that the villagers developed a growing consciousness of the use that could be made of the institutions of the law. The idea that the community was somehow static or docile was certainly mistaken in relation to the period in which Thom wrote. I have attempted here to show that the community was in a far more vibrant state of development than he suggested.

The most obvious influence on the character of the villagers was their relationship with the sea. It is completely wrong to suggest that the fishermen were always very poor. They were never very wealthy, by any stretch of the imagination, but some were financially comfortable – one may think of the example of James Gowans who died in 1800 and left his family fifty pounds sterling. But it was always the sea that dictated the prosperity of the villagers. (A local person's thoughts might turn to the motto of the town of Montrose – *"Mare ditat, rosa decorat"* – translated as *"the sea enriches, the rose adorns."*) Apart from the reference to the rose, the same was true for Gourdon. When the fishing failed, the fishermen turned to trade; and they were successful, for a time, as traders. Mysteriously, it would appear that the Gowan family effectively ceased trading in the early nineteenth century. It is not clear why, but the fact that James Gowan, son of Robert Gowan and Ann Criggie, died bankrupt in 1806 may have had a bearing on this. There was, at times, real hardship in the village; and when the menfolk did not return after a storm, their widows and children could look only to the Kirk to keep them clothed and fed – the story of the notorious Storm of Wind in 1730 provides ample evidence of this, were it needed. On the other hand, success could also breed change for the better; increasing numbers of male villagers were able to read and write by the end of the eighteenth century, and in the early nineteenth century some even bought their own homes from the local laird. Therefore, while poverty was never far away, one cannot simply think of very poor fishermen merely subsisting on their earnings. That picture is enshrined in tradition because many did indeed experience poverty on that scale – no one can deny that either – but it is only half of the truth, especially towards the end of the eighteenth century.

Thom's notion that the villagers were not really troubled by religion is also untenable. An interest in the relationship they had with the Christian faith is evident from the earliest times. I have frequently cited the incidents of 1676 and 1714 as evidence supporting this conclusion; one should not be fooled by the increase of litigation and the decline in the exercise of authority on the part of the Kirk Session as evidence that Thom's statement, while untrue in the earlier period, was correct by the late eighteenth century – it was not. I have argued that, in order to understand the religious character of the villagers in this time, one must first look to the ministry of Thomas Dow and the relationship that he sought to establish through this ministry with his parishioners. He seems to have had some success in co-operating with the villagers; this does show that a good relationship was fostered between the minister and his "flock." Most telling of all, perhaps, in this context, is the court process of *Walker and Jeamie v Milne and Allan* (1778), in which the villagers still looked to the Kirk as the authority to denounce those who had (allegedly) caused harm to their neighbours. The Kirk was right at the heart of the way in which the community defined itself. While this seems to have created elements among the population who were perhaps akin to Burns's *"unco' guid,"* one cannot be sure what influence the church had on some of the other villagers. It does appear, however, that many responded to the minister's request that they should not go to sea on the Sabbath, as the Kirk Session minutes reveal only two breaches of this command, early in Dow's ministry. Certainly in the nineteenth century many of the villagers became very deeply committed Christians.

The relationship that the villagers had with the courts is also instructive. The case involving James Mowat in 1772 shows that the local population cared about more than mere economic ties; but no one can deny that commerce and trade were becoming increasingly important to them. They looked to the courts to regulate those relationships that the Kirk could not. But occasionally, when hard-pressed by unfavourable circumstances, the members of the community were quite willing to take the necessary steps to remedy perceived social wrongs, as in the case of the Meal Mob Riots and in the subsequent tradition pertaining to the release of the womenfolk of the village from prison. One could easily make too much of the popular protests of 1676, 1714 and 1778; but one cannot deny either that they demonstrate collective organisation on the part of the villagers to the end of achieving some common goal. And perhaps this in itself helps us to refute Thom's final comment – that the people of Gourdon were not concerned with politics. It is true that there is no evidence to show that anyone in the village had even heard of Paine or Burke. But the people in the community were fully aware of *local* politics, and when they deemed it necessary they were quite willing to intervene to protect what interests they had in a given situation.

In conclusion, what picture of these villagers can we say emerges? Their livelihoods depended on the sea; poverty was never far away, but some inhabitants of Gourdon did manage, as illustrated by the stories of the Gowans, to succeed in the various trades in which they were involved – and commercial and economic relationships increasingly did matter to them. The Kirk stood right at the heart of the community, as one would expect in a late eighteenth century Scottish village. The people of Gourdon looked to it with a degree of respect, at least in matters relating to the resolution of disputes amongst the villagers; and, judging by the later impact the Christian faith was to have on many of the inhabitants of Gourdon, I am sure it is not too much a leap of the imagination to suggest that some may have taken spiritual succour from the ministry at Bervie – especially, I would propose, in the time of Rev. Dow. A consciousness of the usefulness of the courts in the solution of disputes did grow amongst the villagers; and at times we find that details of specific court cases offer a fascinating insight into the characters of the villagers –they "spring to life" – for example, James Gowan, who seems to have removed every essential piece of equipment from his boat before handing it over to the purchaser thereof, not wishing to deliver all of the goods until paid in full; James Mowat, who genuinely seems to have tried to act in the best interests of one of his fellow villagers; Margaret Jeamie, possibly one of the *unco' guid*; the defiant Agnes Gowan, with her remarkably inventive curses; Alexander Gowan, who was creative with the truth to try to ensure the dismissal of the local tidesman, and so to allow the smuggling trade to thrive again; Mary Bang and Jean Ravel (enough said!); and Janet Alexander, the servant of the Laird of Arbuthnott whose espionage initiated a riot. And let us not forget Robert Gowan, whose temper nearly resulted in his son being pressed into the Royal Navy! These conclusions, these cameos of people long forgotten, placed into the context of the community in which they lived and worked, have inspired this retelling of the story of their lives. In a way, it would not have been wrong to have dedicated this work to all of the people of Gourdon, past and present. But I felt it most fitting of all to dedicate this work to the three Gowan sisters – Margaret, May and Annie – who seem to have taken such pleasure in simply telling the stories of their forebears, and to Annie Pittock, who in turn took such pleasure in telling many of them to me. It is hoped that this story will help to preserve the memory of the community of Gourdon, and to inspire some sense of the significance of the living heritage of the village today.

BIBLIOGRAPHY

As indicated in the footnotes, various sources were consulted in the preparation of this work. These are indicated below. For the sake of convenience I have divided the sources consulted into primary and secondary sources. I present the primary sources in the following format:

The record in question; the reference number thereof; where it may be found

Primary Sources

1. Kirk Session Records/Old Parish Registers/Other Church Records

   1. Inverbervie Kirk Session Records 1648-1800; NAS Ref. CH2/34/1, 2, 6, 7, 9, 10-16, 20; available in the National Archives of Scotland, Princes Street, Edinburgh
   2. Inverbervie Old Parish Registers 1642-1854; NAS Ref. RD 254; available at Inverbervie Library, at Stonehaven Library, at the National Archives of Scotland and at the Aberdeen and North East of Scotland Family History Society Research Centre, King Street, Aberdeen
   3. Kinneff and Catterline Old Parish registers 1616-1854; NAS Ref. RD 262; available at Inverbervie Library, Stonehaven Library, at the National Archives of Scotland and at the Aberdeen and North East of Scotland Family History Society Research Centre
   4. Fetteresso Old Parish Registers; NAS Ref. RD 258; available at Inverbervie Library, at Stonehaven Library, at the National Archives of Scotland and at the Aberdeen and North East of Scotland Family History Society Research Centre
   5. Episcopalian Records of the Church of St James the Great, Stonehaven; available at Aberdeen and North East of Scotland Family History Society Research Centre

2. Court Records

   1. St Andrews Commissary Court Testaments; NAS Ref. CC20/4/27-28; available at the National Archives of Scotland
   2. Brechin Commissary Court Testaments; NAS Ref. CC3/3/6; available at the National Archives of Scotland
   3. Stonehaven Sheriff Court Records; NAS Ref. SC5/8; NAS Ref. SC5/4; NAS Ref. SC5/1/2; available at the National Archives of Scotland
   4. Montrose Burgh Court Records (see case-list below); M/P/15/29/47; M/P/15/148/7; M/P/15/108/1; available at Angus Archives
   5. Hallgreen Barony Court Records (see case-list below); NAS Ref. RH11/35/1; available at the National Archives of Scotland

3. Court Cases

   1. *Alexander v Gowans* (1790) NAS Ref. SC5/8/135
   2. *Barry v Jamie* (1794) M/P/15/108/1
   3. *Bruce v Criggie or Gowan and Gowan* (1787) NAS Ref. SC5/8/116
   4. *Crab v Gowans* (1807) NAS Ref. SC5/8/200

5. *Crombie v Mearns* (1745) NAS Ref. SC5/4
6. *Gowans v Wyse's Executor* (1733) M/P/15/148/7
7. *Grant v Gowans* (1787) NAS Ref. SC5/8/115
8. *Jamie v Watt* (1772) M/P/15/148/7
9. *Law and Watt v Jamie and Mearns* (1753) NAS Ref. SC5/8/50
10. *Arthur Massie* (1668) NAS Ref. RH15/37/119
11. *Mearns and Todd* (1618) as cited in R. Gove, *Gourdon in the Nineteenth Century* (see below)
12. *PF Stonehaven v Fatt and Fatt* (1654) NAS Ref. SC5/1/2
13. *Smith v Gowans* (1787) NAS Ref. SC5/8/116
14. *Walker and Jeamie v Milne and Allan* (1778) NAS Ref. SC5/8/93
15. *Wilson v Lownie* (1777) NAS Ref. SC5/8/92

4. Customs Records

1. Montrose Customs Records; CE53/1/1-3, 6-14; CE53/2/14; available at Dundee City Archives

5. Rait of Hallgreen Papers

1. Papers relating to action between Rait of Halgreen and Viscount Arbuthnott anent salmon fishing on sea shore beneath Inverbervie; NAS Ref. RH15/37/118; available at the National Archives of Scotland
2. Various Writs relating to the port of Gourdon, 1591-1671; NAS Ref. RH15/37/133; available at the National Archives of Scotland
3. Tack of Rait of Hallgreen's Girnel House at Gourdon; NAS Ref. RH15/37/8; available at the National Archives of Scotland
4. List of Inhabitants of Benholm (undated); NAS Ref. RH15/37/192; available at the National Archives of Scotland

6. Printed Transcripts of Primary Sources

1. *Montrose Town Council Minutes*, Volume One; available at Angus Archives
2. *Third Spalding Club Miscellany,* Volume Two; available at Aberdeen Central Library
3. C. S. Terry (ed.) *The Albemarle Papers* (1902)

7. Miscellaneous

1. W. Thom, *Parish of Inverbervie or Bervie,* in Sir John Sinclair (ed.) *Old Statistical Account of Scotland*, Volume XIV – Kincardineshire and South and West Aberdeenshire (1982 Reprint) 136-147; available at Angus Archives and at the National Archives of Scotland (NAS)
2. Erskine, J. *An Institute of the Law of Scotland* Bell & Bradfute, Edinburgh 1871 (New Edition of the 1773 original, J. B Nicolson ed.)
3. Hume, D. *Commentaries on the Law of Scotland Respecting Crimes* The Law Society of Scotland, Edinburgh 1986 reprint
4. MacKenzie, G. *The Laws and Customs of Scotland In Matters Criminal* The Lawbook Exchange Limited, New Jersey 2005 reprint with an introduction by J. Chalmers, C. Gane and F. Leverick

5. Particular Register of Sasines for Kincardineshire; NAS Ref. RS7/5/5; available at the National Archives of Scotland
6. *Montrose Town Council Minutes*, Volume One; available at Angus Archives
7. *Bervie Cess Book*; A copy is available at Bervie Library
8. Papers of the Barclay Allardices; NAS Ref. GD49/399; available at the National Archives of Scotland
9. Rental of Hallgreen (1769); NAS Ref. SC5/76/29; available at the National Archives of Scotland
10. Rental of Hallgreen (1724); NAS Ref. CS96/1/61; available at the National Archives of Scotland

Secondary Sources

1. Adams, D.G. et al. *The Port of Montrose: A History of its Harbour, Trade and Shipping* Hutton Press, Tayport 1993 (available at Angus Archives)
2. Andersen, J. *The Black Book of Kincardineshire* Lewis Smith and Son, Aberdeen 1879 (available at Angus Archives)
3. Black, G. F. *The Surnames of Scotland* Birlin, Edinburgh 1999 (first published 1946 by New York Public Library)
4. Devine, T.M. *The Scottish Nation 1700-2000* Penguin, 1999
5. Dorward, D. *Scottish Surnames* The Mercat Press, 2002
6. Dobson, D. *Mariners of Aberdeen and Northern Scotland* (available at Stonehaven Library)
7. Forte, A. D. M. and Meston, M. C. *Legal Life in Aberdeen in the Late Seventeenth and Early Eighteenth Century – The Aberdeen Stylebook of 1722* in *The Aberdeen University Review,* Vol. LIX, 3, No. 207
8. Fraser, D. *Montrose Before 1700* Montrose: Standard Press, Montrose 1967
9. Fraser, W. *Papers from the Collection of Sir William Fraser* Published for the Scottish History Society, Third Series, Volume Five, 1924
10. Gostwick, M. & F. *Hugh Miller's Cottage* National Trust for Scotland, 1994
11. Gove, R. *Gourdon in the Nineteenth Century* 1980s; published locally
12. Gowans, R. *The Gowans,* in R. Souter (ed.) *Gourdon and the Surrounding Area – A Compilation of Information and Essays on Local History* (unpublished)
13. The IGI (www.familysearch.org)
14. Maxwell, et al. (ed.) *Pre-1855 Gravestones – Kincardineshire* Scottish Genealogy Society, 1986 (available at ANESFHS)
15. McNeill, P. G. and MacQueen, H. L. (ed.) *Atlas of Scottish History to 1707* University of Edinburgh, Edinburgh 1996
16. Miller, J. *Salt in the Blood* Canongate, Edinburgh 1999
17. Scott, H. *Fasti Ecclesiae Scoticanae: Synods of Fife, Angus and Mearns* Oliver and Boyd, Edinburgh 1925, Volume V
18. Souter, R. (ed.) *Gourdon and the Surrounding Area – A Compilation of Information and Essays on Local History* (unpublished)
19. Souter, R. *A Wild and Rocky Coast* Stonehaven
20. Taylor, L.B. (ed.) *Aberdeen Shorework Accounts 1596-1670* Aberdeen, 1972
21. Whatley, C. *Scottish Society 1707-1830* Manchester University Press, 2000
22. Wilkins, F. *The Smuggling of the Northern Shores* 1995 (available at ANESFHS)

APPENDIX ONE:
PRE-1800 GOURDON WILLS

TESTAMENT TESTAMENTAR OF WILLIAM JAFFRAY
NATIONAL ARCHIVES OF SCOTLAND (NAS) Ref. CC3/3/6
August 1655

The testament test[ament]ar l[atte]re will legacie and Inventar[y] of the goods geir debts sommes of money of umqle William Jaffray in Gourdine within the parochine of Bervie the tyme of his deceis who deceist in the month of August jaj vjc fyftie fyve yeiris faithfully maid and given upe be his awen mouth ____ ____ nominates of his exe[cuto]rs and dispositione of his guidis and gear And that in presens of John Barras Nottar in Bervie William Rait Elder of Hallgreen William Naper of Harvieston and of the ____ ____ and persons following.

In primis the said defunt hade in his possessione the tyme fors[ai]d thrie no[l]t estimat to xiij lib price of the present Inde [?] £x Item ane hors with his ganging gear estimat to xx lib Item fyve young nolt all estimat to xl lib Item sawine in the ground of aittis fyve bollis estimat to the thrid Item fyften bolls at iij lib the boll Inde xli lib Item sowen of bear six bolls estimat to the fourth curnt Inde twentie four bolls at £iij vjs viijd ye boll Inde Lxxx lib Item the utencill and domiceill of hes hous estimat at to £xiij vjs viijd

> Summa of ye Inventarie ------------------------------ ijc xliij lib vjs viijd
> Ffollows ye debts awand to the deid
> Item be Robert Wattsone in Hillsyde of Bervie xl lib Item be Alexr Brawne in

Clousburne x lib xiijs iiijd

> Summa of the debts awand to the deid ------------ L lib xiijs iiijd
> Summa of the Inventarie and debts ---------------- ijc Lxxxxiiij lib
> No debts awend be ye deid
> The f[o]r[e]s[ai]d gear being davydit in thrie partis Ilk p[a]rt is Lxxxxviij lib
> Ffollowes the legacie

Item the said William Jaffray being seik in body but perfect in soul and memorie submettes his soull to God frae ____ ____ hoping in faiff throw the meritts of Jesus Christ his savior And ordaines his body to be honestly buried in the Kirkyard of Bervie Item he nominates Robert Alexr Catherine Agnes and Margaret Jaffray his ba[i]rnes exe[cuto]rs to him And nominats Robert Jaffray Elder his father Robert Jaffray Youner and John Jaffray his brothers Alexr Mill Elder his father in law Alexr Mill James Mill his goodbrethren Tutors to ____ his said children in respect of ____ and lesseage to sie them wiell governit and brought upe And nominats and appoints the abovewrettine William Raitt of Halgreine and William Naper of Harvestone ____ to sie his barnes weill guydit.

The rest of the will deals simply with its execution. Jon Barclay was the Notary Public who dealt with the will.

TESTAMENT UMQLE JOHN LARGIE
NAS Ref. CC20/4/27/221-222
17th September 1793

The testament dative and Inventory of the goods gear and debts of umqle John Largie Shipmaster in Gurdon within the parish of Bervie and Sherrifdom of <u>blank</u> the time of his death which was upon the <u>blank</u> day of <u>blank</u> one thousand seven hundred eighty years faithfully made and given up by James Largie in Gurdon father of the said defunt and Executor Dative qua nearest of him decerned to him after due citation by Public Edict + C. By Decreet of the Commissary of St Andrews dated the fifth day of August seventeen hundred and eighty nine years The said Executor gives up for confirmation the sum of five pounds sterling due and resting to the said Defunct by John Walker late in Newton now in Chapleton and Francis Logie late in Crawton now in Uras Conllie and Seallie for time by account with interest of said sum from and after the <u>blank</u> day of December mijc and eighty seven being six months after the delivery of said time and till paid specified and contained in a Decreet of the Sherrif Substitute of Kincardineshire at the said Defuncts instance against them dated the twelfth day of August seventeen hundred and ninety years Item the dues of Extracting the said Decree as the same should be accertained by the Sherrif Court of the said County

Summa Inventary patet

The foregoing Testament was confirmed upon the seventeenth day of September seventeen hundred and ninety three years And George Walker Writer in Stonehaven is become Cautioner for the said Executor.

TESTAMENT UMQLE JAMES GOWANS
NAS Ref. CC20/4/28
21st July 1800

The testament dative and inventory of the goods gear and debts of umqll James Gowans Shipmaster in Gourdon within the parish of Bervie and shire of Mearns the time of his death which was upon the (blank) day of (blank) one thousand (blank) years faithfully made and given up be Ann Alexander Isabell and Christian Gowans all in Gourdon lawful children of the said defunct and Executors Dative qua nearest of him deceased to him (after due citation by public Edict) By decreet of the Commisary of St Andrews dated the eighteenth day of July One thousand eight hundred years.

The said executors give up for confirmation the sum of fifty pounds still due to the said Defunct by the Aberdeen Banking Company confirm to them receipt dated the (blank) day of (blank) one thousand years Summa the interest due thereon

Summa Inventory Putit

The foregoing Testament was confirmed upopn the twenty first day of July One thousand eight hundred years and Peter Christian writer in Stonehaven is become cautioner for the said Executors.

(Extracted from the Register of Testaments held by St Andrews Commissary Court at the National Archives of Scotland in October 2001.)

Note: This James Gowans would seem to be the same as James Gowan, born in 1739, son of John (Jock) Gowan, Fisher in Gourdon. He was therefore the brother of Robert Gowan, Shipmaster in Gourdon, who married Ann Criggie. They in turn were the parents of Alexander Gowan, father of Robert Gowan, father of Margaret Gowan (Joseph Craig's wife), Ann Gowan (Alexander Moncur's wife) and May Gowan (Andrew Lownie's wife).

APPENDIX TWO:
NEGLECTED BERVIE CHRISTENINGS

In NAS Ref. CH2/34/9, there are some fragments of christenings and marriages at Bervie, mostly in the 1660s, which do not appear on the IGI. These have been extracted and a shorthand copy is below. It is **not** in its original order, and is certainly not complete.

a.s.n. – a son named
a.d.n. – a daughter named
m. – married

1664
25 Jul. – John Sutor in Bervie + Elspet Jaffray a.s.n. David

1665
21st Feb. – James Kermock in Bervie m. Elizabeth Mill in Arbuthnott
6th Mar. – John Kermacke in Bervie m. Elizabeth Wright, daughter to Rev. Wm Wright in Bervie
8th May – Wm Cooke in Barnhill m. Issobell Sparkin in Peattie
8th May – Thomas Fatt in Gourdon m. Issobell Geimie in Gourdon
28th May – Alexander Shepherd in Benholm m. Jean Watt in Gourdon
1st June – Andro Jeamie in Gourden m. Barbra Blewhouse [Blewhas – Blews??]
14th June – John Mearns in Bervie m. Isobell Lawe in Benholme
20th June – Androwe Crookshank in Caterlein m. Margrit Wyllie in Bervie
24th June – Andrew Thomson in Einglishgrieg [St Cyrus] m. Margaret Jaffray in Bervie
13th Sep. – John Geimie [Jeamie] + Issobell Gowans in Gourdon a.s.n. John
4th Oct. – Robert Fettus Mill of Peattie + Margaret Bruce a.d.n. Isobel
11th Oct. – Robert Leper sometime in Freewalls now in Bervie + Isobel Cai a.d.n. Margarit
10th Nov. – Dame Catherine Arbuthnott + Viscount Arbuthnott a.d.n. Elizabeth
22nd Nov. – James Cant in Bervie+ Jannet Watt a.s.n. William, Godparents William Kermack and Willima Cant, brother to James above
14th Dec. – James Burgess in Bervie and Barbara Dickie a.d.n. Margarit (begotten in fornication).

1666
14th Jun. – Andro Garvie, Town of Bervie m. Issobell Donaldson, Town of Bervie
5th Jul. – Robert Gemie in Eiglishgreig m. Margaret Watt Bervie
12th Jul. – James Memii in Benholme m. Janet Leper in Bervie
6th Dec. – James Taylloure in Barnehill + Jean Marshall a.s.n. Robert

1667
Jan. 20th – Robert Cook in Burnsyde + Janet Rinken a.d.n. Jannett
Jan. 24th – James Cant in Bervie + Jannet Man a.s.n. James James Willock Yor. Alexander Man and James Burgess being Godfathers
Feb. 9th – Robert Keith in Barnehill + Anne Nicoll a.s.n. Robert
Feb. 18th – Robert Petrie in Gourdon + Catherine Stott a.s.n. James
Mar. 8th – Andrew Smith in Hillside m. Janet Crowe in Arbuthnott

Mar. 13th – Robert Hanton in Bervie + Isobell Duncan a.d.n. Jannett
Apr. 14th – William Dickie in Arbuthnott m. Issobell Robertsone in Bervie
Apr. 15th – Andro. Arbuthnott in Bervie + Jannet Glennie a. s. n. Robert
Aug 18th – Androw Robertson in Bervie + Girsall Allardes a.s.n. Allexander
Aug 24th – Wm Mollyson flesher in Bervie + Isobell Dickie a.s.n. William
Aug 25th – John Meldrum in Hillsyde + Catherine Preshone a.d.n. Anna
Dec. 11th – John Bruce in Bervie + Margaret Stotte a.d.n. Anna
Dec. 11th – Walter Warden att Milne of Bervie + Margaret Mill a.s.n. William

1668
6th May – Patrick Reid in Benholm m. Margaret Spence in Bervie
6th May – David Richie alias Fatt in Gourdon m. Margaret Geimie in Gourdon
5th Aug. – Andro Thomson in Einglishgreig m. Margaret Jaffray in Gourdon daughter to Thomas Jaffray
5th Oct. – John Sutor Gourdon m. Elspit Jaffray, lawful eldest daughter to Thomas Jaffray in Gourdon

1669
3rd Jan. – George Stoit in Silliflatt + Annas Willock a.d.n. Margarit
22nd Feb. – John Lamb in Bervie + Margaret Hebron a.s.n. James
22nd Mar. – Andro Arbuthnott in Bervie and Janet Glennie a.s.n. James
4th Apr. – Thomas Richie alias Fatt in Gourdon + Issobell Geimie a.d.n. Margarit
14th May – Alexr Mann in Bervie + Elpset Burgess a.d.n. Anna

A new book for recording christenings and marriages was begun by the Session Clerk in 1671. As stated above, all of the above fragments of the old book are now incorporated into NAS Ref. CH2/34/9.

APPENDIX THREE:
LIST OF BENHOLM INHABITANTS
(*MID-1600s*).

Rait of Hallgreen Family Papers
NAS Ref. RH15/37/192

Below is a list of inhabitants of Benholm Parish, Kincardineshire, in the early seventeenth century. Although undated, the names of some of the Heritors on the list act as a form of dating and these, with further research, will help to pinpoint a more exact date for the list, within about a margin of ten years or so. The purpose of the list itself is not clear. The fact that the list crosses estates would suggest that it is not a roll of any one set of tenants. The fact too that it mentions no taxes or rents would infer that the list was not a tax roll or for collecting the rents due to the Lairds. This basically leaves one of two obvious possibilities – firstly, that it was compiled by the Kirk to give a listing of the heads of households eligible to participate in the election of the minister for Benholm. However, this is also unlikely as the list specifies that some of the inhabitants were unable to complete some sort of duty because of illness – being "sickly" – or because they were unwilling so to do – hence the "runaways." The second possibility is that this was a roll of fencible men in Benholm Parish. This would allow for the fact that some men were described as being unable to fulfil the duty concerning which the list was compiled. It would also help to understand the concept of "runaway" – someone who, for whatever reason, did not want to fight. This would also explain the fact that it crosses the estates of several landowners – the Lundies, the Ramsays, the Raits and the Barclays of Johnston being among these. The obvious question then must be as to why a roll of fencible men was taken. The answer may be very simple – if the list was taken in the first half of the seventeenth century, as the style of handwriting and cross-referencing with other records of the time suggest – then this may have been the response of the Benholm heritors to the signing of the National Covenant. With such a powerful local magnate as the Earl Marischall being on the side of the Covenanters, it would have been essential for the smaller Lairds to "do their bit" as well. This would place the list as having been taken around 1639, when the Covenant was signed, prompting the Civil War. To ascertain whether or not any of these men actually fought in the Civil War would require investigation first of the involvement in the War of the Heritors on the list. The list does show that 194 men were originally thought to be at the disposal of the Heritors.

However, many of these names were later struck off, either because the men were "runaways," or too "weake" or "sickly" to fight. One was even described as being too "young," suggesting that there was a humanity to the Benholm Heritors that meant that they would not send someone they considered too young (presumably in his early teens) to fight. Equally the "old" were excused.

On a genealogical note there are also some interesting points. Firstly, the list of seaman, which would seem to be exclusively from Johnshaven, is a fairly long list, showing that the village was a thriving fishing port in the seventeenth century. Secondly, the names of the fishermen, some of which eventually migrated to neighbouring Gourdon, are also of interest. For example, from this list, the Criggie family of Gourdon clearly originated from Johnshaven (and also from the evidences of the Bervie OPRs, which show that no Criggies were in Bervie Parish prior to the first decade of the eighteenth century, while there were plenty of them in Benholm earlier on). The Blews and the Mearns family were also clearly very old residents of Johnshaven, as were the Souters. Thirdly, the names of the farm-folk clearly include all classes of people, from the landed gentry to the cottars. This is the only reasonable way to explain the long lists of people for places like Arbirnie and Knoxes – they cannot all have been tenant farmers. In terms of establishing relationships between the people on the farms, caution is required – while people on each farm with the same surname may have some relationship, the concept of "Elder" and "Younger" does not always infer "father" and "son" – merely that the distinction between two people of the same name was made by comparing their ages.

Finally, the list was transcribed from a list held in the National Archives of Scotland, in the Rait of Hallgreen Papers (NAS Ref. RH15/37/192), which is stored out of the main building, and so anyone wishing to consult the original would have to order the document from Edinburgh two to three working days before their visit. As far as possible I have tried to transcribe the names with the original (not "corrected") spellings. Some names, however, escape me and I have denoted these with a blank thus – "____." Many of these are difficult to read because, as the men became unsuited to being on the roll their names were struck through. Such names are indicated with an asterisk thus – "*." Some names also appear, when transcribed, strange in their construction – these are marked with a double question mark, as the transcription may, actually, be wrong.

Knoxes:- Harie Barclay [of Johnston?], James Feltus, Rot King*, Alexr Cant, William Andrew*, Rot Watsone, Andro Stoddie, Andro Jack*, And. Walker, James Lawrence, Rot. Cant*, Alexr. Clerk, Wm Middleton, Alexr Mill Elder ab, James Mill ab, Alexr Mill Younger ab, James Brown, James Lyon*, Wm H____*, James Kep, Jon Barid, Andrew Barid, Alexr Barid

Neather Benholm:- Mr. Alexr Wood, Wm Anderson*, Jon Watt, Roger Syratt*, Andrew Cant*, Wm Young, David Marins, Johne Marins

Over Benholme:- Sir James Ramsay, Geo. Ramsay, And. Ramsay*, Jon Durward, Wm Walker, John Nauchtie, Rot. Stephen*, Alexr Craig, Wm Lyndsay, Andro Hay*, Robt Craw/Croll??, Wm Traill

Temple:- James Betie*, Andrew Edward, David Findlay

Forgie:- Wm Ross Elder*, Alexr Rosse, Wm Rosse, Thomas Kaird, Jon Barid

Greenleyis:- ____ Wobster*, Malcolme Fleair??*

Luchmedden:- Rot. Keit[h?], Geo Petrie, John Dalbuie??, James Hamptonne

Tullo:- John Stratone, Wm Browne*, Andro Barclay, Francis Lundie, David Watsone, Wm Ogilvie

Kirktonne:- Rot Wallace, Rot Kennie*, Rot Bruce, David Watt*, Wm Watt*, Alexr Allane*

Qukstonne??:- Geo. Watsone, Walter Greig, Wm Greig

Arbirnie:- Alexr Barclay, David Barclay, Mr. John Barclay, Geo Rot, Walter Wilsone James Crowddale*, Alexr Cant, John Lyon, Alexr Lairgy, James Brown, Alexr Tailyeour, Adam Petrie*, James Keit[h?]*, John Kerne*

Stane of Benholme:- Andro Lundie, David Mcoll?? Younger, James Willock, David ____, Elder, David Symsone, James Betrie, Rot Smith, Wm Betie, Andro Betie, David Morice, Geo. Loch, Henrie Ennerdaill, Rot Marchtie, Jon Yonnie, Alexr Kerrie*, Geo Kerne*, Alexr Souter*, Alexr Wylie, Wm Cuthbert, Wm Jamie

Quhytfield:- James Presehor, Alexr Tweddale

Ballandro:- Wm Rait, James Wallace, Alexr Rot, Wm Rot*, James Mitchell*, Wm Baird*, James Baird*, Alexr Kraftie*, Jon Hamptionne, Alexr Nicoll, Jon Cowie

Brethertonne:- Francis Keit[h?], Alexr Keit[h?]*, Patrick Greig, Thomas Clerk, James Hall, Jon _____*, David Law, David Smith*, Andro Watt, James Marnie, David Nicoll, James Beattie, James Merch*, Rot Clerk*

Land People of Jonshaven:- Rot Lyon, Thomas Lumchanane, Wm Lyon, _____ Baird*, Wm Burgess*, Jon Maich_____??, Rot Clerk, Jon Andersone a sor leg, Andrew Brawn*, James Bran*, Jon Reid Elder Nor so??, Geo Souter, Rot Buchanane, Rot Chapmain??*, Wm Mill*, James Wilsone*

Seamen 1:- [Divisions probably represent different boats] David Ritchie*, Rot Blewhes,* Jon Traile, Alexr Blewes*, Jon Mill, David Ritchie Yngr*

Seamen 2:- Wm Law, Wm Merins, Alexr Blewes, James Kerd*, John Fouler, Jon Tod*

Seamen 3:- Jon Largie, Geo Largie*, David Blewes, Jon Law, Wm Reid*, Jon Mernies, Alexr Reid a runaway

Seamen 4:- Rot Allane old, Geo Allane Elder, Patrick Traill* weake, Rot Allane Yngr*, John Brigfoord, Rot Liske* Sickly, Jon Reid*, And. Morrice*

Seamen 5:- David Merins* old, David Blewhas*, Alexr Craigie, Geo. Annand, Gilbert Law* weake, Gilbert Souter*, Alexr Young

Seamen 6:- Alexr Law, Andro Law sickly, Wm Burgess a ruining leg, Patrick Meldrum blody, Jon Alexander

Seamen 7:- Andro Largie, Alexr Craigie Yngr, Alexr Blewes, Lawrence Oliphant, Jon Morice weak + sickly, Rot Allane* Young

APPENDIX FOUR:
RENTAL OF HALLGREEN (1769)
NAS Ref. SC5/76/29

The below rental is extracted from the Stonehaven Sheriff Court Records. The money referred to is in Scots pounds.
Note: B=Bolls
         F=firlots
         P=pecks (old measurements for bear (barley) and meal).

Rental of the Lands of Hallgreen and Gourdon and Lands of Kinghornie for Cropt 1769

Tenants Names	Bear B/f/p	Meal B/f/p	Money £/s/d
Alexr Christie for the Mains Tack for 19 years from WhitS 1762	53/-/-		104/6/8
Ditto for Hilside	15/-/-		66/13/4
Ditto for Greivesdale, Beuicks + Nether Ward			84/-/-
Ditto for the Garden, but not Contained in the Tack			20/-/-
James Christie for 19 years from WhitS 1766 pays for Mussel Pool	24/-/-		248/-/-
Robt Coutts Tack for 19 years from WhitS 1767 pays for the Keyhead of Gourdon and Martins Haugh, with Teind money	16/-/-		134/13/4
Thomas Christie Tack for 38 years From WhitS 1762 pays for the Lands Called Crossdale			55/-/-
James Strachan no Tack pays for 8 Riggs on the Braehead of Bervie	15/-/-		
Ditto for the School Braes			36/-/-
Geo. Mackie, Tack for 53 years From WhitS 1768 for Dendaudrum	4/-/-	2/-/-	24/-/-
Robt + Geo. Napiers, Tack for 57 Years from WhitS 1757 – pays for 4/9th parts of the Mill of Bervie 87 Bolls of Meall and 18 Bolls of Bear For the Mill Lands But there is 6			

Ffirlotts of the Bear to be discounted
Yearly for upholding the Damm So
That there is only payable   16/2/-   8/2/-

James Watt for the Smiths
Possession, No Tack   4/-/-   2/-/-

James Stiven for his feu in Bervie
And for 2 Riggs called Skitterly £14   32/-/-

John Criggie for a large fishing Boat
With houses and yeards   33/6/8

John Campbell and Wm. King for
The kelp on the rocks   21/-/-
Ditto for the half of a Lobster Chest   6/6/-

House Rent for Gourdon List   43/13/-

              Total   147/2/-   10/2/-   910/19/-

James Allardyce Esqr of that Ilk
For ffour 19 years from WhitS 1759
Pays for a part of Watergates, the
Converted price of 22B. Bear at £6/6
£15/5 And for a Custom Lamb £1/0   16/15/-
        This is the rent by the Tack but it is a part of the Lands Contd in Robert Napiers Tack for which he gets allowance yearly for the 22B. Bear and half a boll of Meal at the the price of the farm Bear sold at £1 Scots for the Lamb

Total for Cropt 1769 except the
Salmond fishing   147/2/-   10/2/-   927/14/-
But there is to be deducted 12/ Scots Stated as paid by Margaret Allan for a house Which is in now given off to Jas Campbell for holding Kelp and the rent dispensed with

                                               -/12/-
                                          927/2/-

Provost Christie is to pay for the
Lands of Kinghornie Cropt 1769   [blank]
The Salmond fishing 1769 is   [blank]

There is payable to the **Minister of Bervie** 6B. Bear + 4 Bolls
2 pecks Meall – and of money   82/16/-
To the **Schoolmaster**   22/-/6
To **Lord Arbuthnott** of few   20/-/-
To the **Ministers of St Andrews** Teind Duty   22/-/
To **Millhouse**   8/-/-
                                      Total 155/8/6

Note: It would seem that the rents for Gourdon were revised several times, hence the case involving Margaret Allan, and the last entry above. What is interesting is that there were feus – probably sub-feus – of property in Gourdon held by the people there. This may explain the story that the Gowans owned their own property for generations in the Lang Close – it was neither outright ownership nor was it tenancy, but a level of tenure in between – a sub-feu. It is also interesting to note that John Criggie (who may have been the same as the father of Ann Criggie who married Robert Gowan in 1755) was the only Gourdon Shipmaster who leased his boat from Hallgreen – the rest of the Gourdon boats must have been owned, by this date, by the Gourdon Skippers.

One further thing to note at this stage is that there survives another rental of the Hallgreen Estate from 1724 (NAS Ref. CS96/1/61). Here only two boats were leased from Hallgreen. Below is the list of tenants; there was much more information on the original about the exact amounts of rent paid by the tenants.

1. George Raitt for Skitterly
2. Robert Hamptoun for the Mains
3. James Dick as depond on by Robt Jaffray the former tenant
4. Thomas Jolly
5. William Linton
6. Agnes Henderson
7. Peter Greig
8. Andrew Stevenson
9. Thomas Strachane
10. Simeon Gibson for his own and George Gait's possession
11. John Watt
12. William Jaffray beside a band of hooks six in the harvest
13. John Cowie
14. Andrew Grieg and John Mories pays for one fish boat £58/13/4 worth of white fish
15. Andrew Jamie for another pays £26/3/4 worth of white fish

This means that, even at this early date, most of the Gourdon boats were owned by the people of the village.

APPENDIX FIVE:
CONSTRUCTING THE GOWAN LINE

Throughout this work I have made various references to the inter-relationships between Gowan family members. I feel, therefore, I should briefly explain the construction of the Gowan line.

I can trace my own line back (using the Statutory Registers) to Alexander Gowan, father of Robert Gowan, who was a whaler, and who was born in 1801. We actually know less about Robert than about his father, Alexander. Much that we know about Robert is built on oral tradition – he was a whaler, and we also know from the census returns that he worked as a fisherman in his later years. In my own family Alexander stood as the earliest ancestor who could be remembered in oral tradition – my great-aunt, Lily Young (nee Christie, sister of my grandfather, Duncan Craig Christie) could just remember the older folk in Gourdon in her younger days speaking about this Alexander Gowan, who would have been her great great grandfather. Lily died in 1997, and managed to pass this information on to me in about 1996. Alexander did not survive to be recorded on the first census in 1841, and so, normally, any line traced back from him would remain just that – theoretical. Fortunately we can, actually, be a bit more certain about his ancestry. Interestingly, my aunt Lily's traditional family line was also remembered in another branch of the family but with two extra generations further back. This was recorded in the notes of Robert Gowans of Gourdon, a Gourdon skipper, whose notes, if I recall correctly, were dated to the 1940s. In the 1980s these were transcribed by Roy Souter, and it is by his kind permission that I use the information contained in them here. Robert Gowans stated that his father, James Gowans, had told him the names of his Gowan line as follows:

Jock (not certain)

father of

Robert (who had a sloop)

father of

Alex

father of

Rob (known as Auld Robert)

father of

Rob (known as Auld Rob, who himself was the father of James)

Robert Gowans managed to identify Auld Robert as Robert Gowan, husband of Margaret Mowat (herself the daughter of John Mowat, son of James Mowat, weaver in Gourdon, who was remembered by my grandmother as "auld Jeems fae Fernyflett" – Auld Jeems was born in Fernyflett farm, son of James Mowat and Christian Lindsay). The statutory registers would easily have carried him back that far. Thus I could see how my line fitted into his line – I descend, on my grandfather's side of the family, from Auld Robert's daughter Margaret Gowan (Mrs. Craig) and on my grandmother's side of the family from his Auld Robert's younger daughter, Ann Gowan (Mrs. Moncur).

First, is the line reliable? We know that it is correct back to Alex, because Auld Robert's death certificate reveals that his parents were Alexander Gowans and Helen Kemlo (they were married in 1798 at Stonehaven Episcopalian Church). Robert Gowans himself said that his father was "not certain" that Jock stood at the head of the line, but he was certain about Robert "who had a sloop." This level of scrutiny of the available material is an indicator of authenticity. Furthermore, we can also say that various other traditions recorded by Gowans are correct. Finally, we must remember that, while the line is fantastic and takes us back a long way today, it did not really take James's family line back that far – only to his great great grandfather, and one more (uncertain) generation beyond that. James was alive in the early twentieth century, so in effect we are looking at a man being able to recount his ancestry back for between one hundred and fifty and two hundred years – this is not that unusual, and it certainly was not unusual in a fishing community, or indeed any Scottish community, where one's ancestry was such an important part of one's heritage. I am utterly convinced that the line is a reliable source. As I shall show, we can, in fact, argue convincingly that Alexander was in fact the son of Robert "who had a sloop."

It is correct to say that there was an Alexander Gowan, son of a Robert Gowan, who was born in 1768, and that Robert was, indeed, a shipmaster and notorious smuggler (from the Customs Records). We may also observe that there was only one Robert Gowan who was fathering children in the parish at that time, the father of the Alexander mentioned who was born in 1768, and he was the husband of Ann Criggie (they were married in 1755). Furthermore, we can identify this Robert as indeed Robert who was fathering children (i.e. we have to exclude the possibility that the man being chased by the customs officer was not simply some Robert in the village who was not fathering children). The Robert in the Customs Records is consistently identified as the skipper of the *Ann* of Gourdon. Firstly, let us note the name of the ship – the *Ann* is almost certainly, when set beside the proposed line, a reference to Ann Criggie, wife of Robert Gowan. Now, there was a dispute in 1792 (see page 32) between Robert, the owner of the *Ann*, and his son Alexander Gowan, who was its skipper. Thus we know that Robert Gowan the skipper had indeed fathered children, and one was called Alexander. But is this Alexander **the** Alexander of the line? The answer to that question is very simply yes, after a glance at the Bervie Old Parish Registers. These would appear to be relatively complete. There was only one Alexander Gowan son of Robert Gowan born at anywhere near the right date in the registers – Alexander Gowan, son of Robert Gowan and Ann Criggie, born in 1768 in Gourdon. What about non-conformists? Could we perhaps be looking at a different Alexander son of a different Robert born in Gourdon but baptised by an Episcopalian minister? Again, the answer is no. There was no non-conformity in Bervie Parish (by non-conformity here I mean outright secession) until the 1790s, and so we are not dealing with a situation where Alexander might have been baptised by an Episcopalian. True, he did marry in an Episcopalian Church, but it is clear that that was because his wife, Helen Kemlo, was probably herself of that particular denomination of the faith. One final question might stand in the way of finally identifying the Alexander of 1768 as the Alexander of the line – what if this Alexander was simply one who moved to Gourdon when he was young from elsewhere, whose father just happened to be called Robert? Such an argument is difficult to counter, but rather nonsensical anyway, when one considers the weight of circumstantial evidence that points to Alexander having had origins in Gourdon and the absolute conviction of oral traditions that he did (rather too many to list here). In short, I really think that it is an utter nonsense to suggest that Alexander of the line was anyone other than Alexander Gowan who was born in 1768, son of Robert Gowan and Ann Criggie. Perhaps if a seaman's ticket for Alexander could be found, giving his date and place of birth, any such doubts that anyone would choose to entertain (without any good cause) could be put to rest. I have not yet ordered this, and there is a good chance that no such document survives. In any case, it is absolutely clear that the line is correct in identifying Alexander Gowan as the son of Robert Gowan and Ann Criggie. To strengthen this link, let us consider the oral tradition that Alexander went to sea with his father in the sloop when he was young. Clearly this is a memory of the shared use of the *Ann* of Gourdon that led to the rift between father and son in the 1790s. Furthermore, we know that the Alexander who definitely was the son of Robert Gowan and Ann Criggie was married – in one action before the Sheriff Court in Stonehaven, dated 1806, reference is made to his wife (frustratingly her name is not mentioned – if it were the link would be unquestionable) and to his siblings. Thus we know that the Alexander who was the son of Robert Gowan and Ann Criggie was married and lived in Gourdon in this period. The conclusion is somewhat obvious – he was indeed the same person as Alexander Gowan who married Helen Kemlo, and so we may with some certainty, based on the records alone, that Alexander Gowan who married Helen Kemlo was the son of Robert Gowan and Ann Criggie.

Let us, then, move a generation back. Robert Gowan and Ann Criggie, again, are an easy couple to spot in both the Kirk Session records (where they are referred to in relation to one another) and elsewhere. Robert can be identified as he is consistently referred to elsewhere as the skipper of the *Ann* of Gourdon. It is true to say that there were two boats called the *Ann* of Gourdon, which confuses matters, but one belonged to James, who was probably Robert's brother (it was sold in the 1790s to Alexander Alexander). We should therefore look at Robert's parentage.

When Robert Gowans wrote out his notes relating to the line in the 1940s he did not have access to many of the sources we have today, (which bears testament to the remarkable ability he had to get things right in spite of the lack of material). He knew that his father had believed that Robert Gowan, who was the husband of Ann Criggie, was the son of Jock Gowan. Who was Jock? Once again, we come down to a rather negative, but nontheless valid, argument. There was a John Gowan who had a son, Robert, born in 1731 (the year after the infamous "Storm of Wind). This is the only Robert Gowan whose birth is recorded in the registers between 1699 and 1757. Thus one might be excused for jumping to the conclusion, and applauded for doing so in light of the oral tradition, that Robert of the line was indeed the same person as Robert Gowan son of John Gowan. Robert again is attributed by the family with origins in Gourdon, for he is described as the son of the keeper of the Shore Inn (hence my identification of this person with Jock). Robert did leave a gravestone, but frustratingly his age is not recorded on it. However, we can say that there was only one active family of Gowans in the village between 1725 and 1755 – that of John Gowans. Why? The answer is simple. There were several Gowan men, who might have gone on to have families, who were killed in the Storm of Wind in 1730. James Gowanie, by tradition the brother of Jock, almost lost his life too up at Roger's Haven, and he left the village without fathering a family there. In short, apart from John, all the male Gowans left the village or died in the early eighteenth century for one reason or another (but mainly these reasons centred on the Storm of Wind). Again, we can ignore the possibility that some Gowans could have been registered at non-conformist establishments, since there is absolutely no non-conformist allegiance known of in the family before 1798. So I think that it is fairly safe to say that James Gowans was right to identify Robert Gowan of the line as Robert Gowan born in 1731, the son of John Gowan.

But there is a complication in saying that we are only dealing with one family of Gowans in the village in this period, because there may possibly have been two John Gowans fathering children in the same period. This is because there were two John Gowans married in 1725 – one married an Isobel Fatt, another a Margaret Lamb, and in this period the baptismal registers do not reveal the name of the mother of the children in question. Either could be the father of Robert Gowan born in 1730, and this is why we really do not know who Robert's mother was. It is just possible that one man, John, could have married one wife earlier in the year, and then she died, and then married the other later in the year, but I do not think this particularly likely – I think that there were two Johns who were married in 1725. But I do not think that they both continued to father children (I grant that this is confusing, but it does all make sense). I think that one John died in the late 1720s or even in the Storm of Wind. This is because there is reference to the birth of a daughter to John Gowan **Younger** in Gourdon in 1726. By implication, therefore, there was a John Gowan **Senior** who was capable of having children. Now, by 1731, with the birth of Robert, the distinction has disappeared – and it is never referred to again. Furthermore, an Isobel Fatt appears on the poor roll soon after and remains there for the rest of her life. My view is (and it could be wrong) that John Gowan husband of Isobel Fatt died before 1731, perhaps in the Storm of Wind. The other John Gowan then was the only male Gowan in the village who was fathering children by 1729. His son Robert (of the line) was born in 1731, and then he had several other children – Alexander (born 1733), John (born 1736), and James (born 1739). I believe that all of these children were the sons of John Gowan and **Margaret Lamb**. The case for such a view is strengthened by the fact that the only daughter that John had was called Margaret, born in 1729. Thus we may suggest that the mother of Robert Gowan of the line was, in fact, Margaret Lamb. But we cannot be sure about this at all – all we can be sure about is that his father was called John Gowan. I am more certain that there was only one male Gowan called John in the village in this period, hence the certainty with which I ascribe the references to a John Gowan in the Kirk Session records to **the** John Gowan of the line, father of Robert Gowan, born in 1731. But again one must remember the outside possibility that there were indeed two John Gowans in the village in this period, which would render it impossible to say that the John referred to in the Kirk Session records is the same person as John Gowan, father of Robert Gowan who married Ann Criggie.

In Chapter Two I made reference to my theories about the origins of the Gowan line. I am quite sure that these are plausible. At present, however, it is impossible to reconstruct the lineage from John Gowan, father of Robert Gowan who married Ann Criggie, back to Jon Gowans, who probably hailed from Montrose. I am content to maintain that the former John is descended from the latter.

APPENDIX SIX:
LINEAGE OF THE AUTHOR

On a final note, I thought it might be apt to add in here my own direct line, back to the Gowans, who have been mentioned throughout this history. I always think it amazing that the family has moved less than thirty miles in their round trip from Montrose to Gourdon and back again in the case of my branch (Montrose is where I now live) in the course of the past four hundred years!

Andrew Robert Craig Simpson, b. 1984, son of

Arthur Edmond Simpson, English teacher in Montrose, b. 1949 and Alison Lilian Christie, French, German and Latin teacher, the latter b. 1947 and the daughter of

Duncan Craig Christie, b. 1904, boat-builder in Montrose, and Jessie Smith Moncur, b. 1904, the latter the daughter of

Robert Moncur, b. 1873, general merchant in Gourdon, and Helen Doig Ramsay, b. 1875, the former the son of

Alexander Moncur, b. 1839, fisher in Gourdon, and Ann Gowan, b. 1845, the latter the daughter of

Robert Gowan, b. 1801, whaler and latterly fisher in Gourdon, and Margaret Mowat (grand-daughter of James Mowat, weaver in Gourdon), Robert having been the son of

Alexander Gowan, b. 1768, shipmaster in Gourdon, and Helen Kemlo, the former the son of

Robert Gowan, b. 1731, shipmaster in Gourdon, and Ann Criggie, the former the son of

John (Jock) Gowan, who was almost certainly descended from Jon Gowans. This last Jon possibly hailed from Montrose, born in the early 1600s, and his wife was one of the Spence family of Gourdon.

(Note – my grandfather, Duncan Craig Christie, was also descended from this line. His mother was Alexanderina Gowans Craig, daughter of Joseph Craig and Margaret Gowans, Margaret herself an elder sister of Ann Gowan (b. 1844) above. Ann's name was spelt both with and without the "e" during the course of her life.)

DROP CHART – LINEAGE OF THE AUTHOR

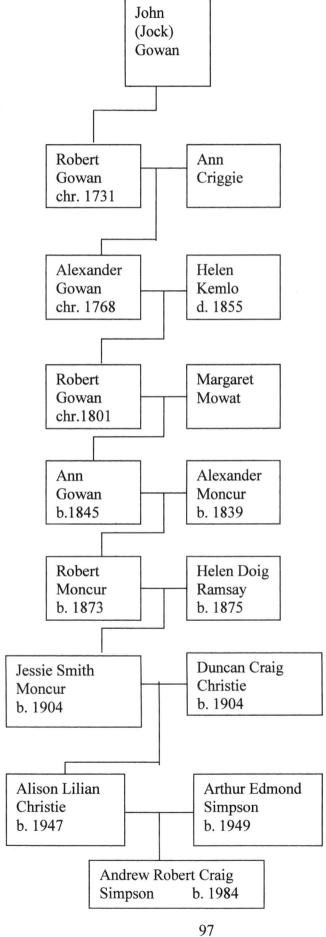

John
(Jock)
Gowan

Robert
Gowan
chr. 1731

Ann
Criggie

Alexander
Gowan
chr. 1768

Helen
Kemlo
d. 1855

Robert
Gowan
chr.1801

Margaret
Mowat

Ann
Gowan
b.1845

Alexander
Moncur
b. 1839

Robert
Moncur
b. 1873

Helen Doig
Ramsay
b. 1875

Jessie Smith
Moncur
b. 1904

Duncan Craig
Christie
b. 1904

Alison Lilian
Christie
b. 1947

Arthur Edmond
Simpson
b. 1949

Andrew Robert Craig
Simpson   b. 1984

INDEX

A

Aberdeen Banking Company	37
Aberdeen Infirmary	60
Alexander, Alexander	35-37
Alexander, Janet	72
Alexander, William	49
Allan, David	44-45
Allan, Janet (fl. 1778)	69-73
Allan, Janet (fl. 1732)	44-45
Allan, Jean	73
Allan, Katherine (Mrs Gowan)	40
Allan, Margaret	45
Alison, Colin (Montrose Writer)	66-67
Anderson, John	11, 64
Annan, Margaret	44
Arbuthnott Family	2, 48, 72-73
Arbuthnott, Rev. James	42
Armada, Story of the	3
Arnott, Rev. William	43-47

B

Bankton (Legal Writer)	66
Barry, James, in Stonehaven	67
Beattie, Baillie	57
Blews Family (note)	11
Blews, Christian (fl. 1751)	50, 58
Blews, Christian (fl. 1778)	73
Blews, Thomas	45
Bruce, Alexander, in Montrose	68
Buchanan, William	33
Burness, William	39

C

Carmelite Friary, Bervie	38
Catterline	35
Chalmers, Rev. William	40
Christie Family (note)	19
Clackmannan	31
Clark, Robert	44
Colvin, Martha	73
Cormack Family (note)	11
Cormak, Elspeth	45
Coull Family (note)	19
Craig Family (note)	19
Craig, Joseph	15
Crawton	22
Criggie, Ann (Mrs Gowan)	5, 50, 57, 68, 76
Criggie, Ann (Mrs Mearns)	73
Criggie, Anna	44-45
Criggie, David	49

C (Cont.)

Criggie, John	44-45
Criggie, Margaret (fl. 1797)	5, 50-51
Criggie, Margaret (Mrs Gowan)	73
Croll, Rev. Robert	50
Cumberland, Duke of	47
Customs Officers	32-35

D

Dickie, Robert (fl. 1730)	44
Dickie, Robert (Councillor)	58
Discipline System	38-51
Doers, John (Montrose Baillie)	65
Dorrit, Elspet	40
Dow, Rev. Thomas	46-63
Draper, Lieutenant	48
Dysart	28, 31

E

Ecclesiastical History	38-62
Discipline	38-51
Welfare	56-62
Education	58-59
Erskine (Legal Writer)	66, 71, 72
Elgin, Lord	68

F

Fatt Family (alias Ritchie)	10
Fatt, David (fl. 1654)	11, 64
Fatt, David (fl. 1674)	40
Fatt, David (fl. 1676)	23, 40
Fatt, Isobel	57
Fatt, Thomas (fl. 1654)	11, 64
Fatt, Thomas (fl. 1678)	41
Fatt, Thomas (fl. 1750)	49
Fishing	21-26
Fraser, John, in Montrose	66
Freeman Family	14
Freeman, Alexander	15, 25
Freeman, James	49
Freeman, Robert	50, 58
Fremane, John	15

G

Garvie, Andrew	40
Gibb, Robert	44, 49
Gillespie, Alexander	58
Gourdon – Name	1
Early History	1-8, 22
Families	9-20
Yorkshire Connections	12
Gove Family (note)	19

G (cont.)

Gove, George	44
Gove, Isobel	45
Gowan(s) Family	15-19
Traditions	28-30
Genealogy (see Appendix 5)	29-30
St Monance Connections	29
Gowan, Agnes	10, 44-45, 65, 70
Gowan, Alexander	32, 35-37, 73
Gowan, Alexander (c. 1768)	5, 34-35, 37
Gowans, Anne (Mrs Moncur)	35, 39
Gowan, David Douglas	75
Gowan, Isobel (d. 1784)	32
Gowan, James (fl. 1797)	5, 50, 76
Gowan, James (d. 1800)	32, 35-37, 72
Gowan, James (c. 1706)	29, 58
Gowan, Jock (John)	24, 30-31, 46
Gowan, John (c. 1756)	24, 68
Gowans, Jon (fl. 1646)	14, 17, 28
Gowan, Margaret (Mrs Craig)	2-3
Gowans, Margaret	65
Gowans, Robert (Historian)	3
Gowan, Robert (c. 1731)	5, 24, 31-32, 34, 35, 50, 51, 68, 76
Gowan, Robert, in Montrose	16
Gowans, "Codlin'" Robert	5
Greig, Jean	45, 59

H

Haddock Fishing	25
Hallgreen Barony Court	64, 65
Healthcare	59-60
Hodge, John	44
Holland	28

J

Jacobitism	42; 47-48
Jaffray Family	2
Jaffray, William	39
James IV	2
James VI	27
Jamie/Jeamie Family	9; 11-13
Jamie, Alexander	66
Jeamie, Andrew (fl. 1750)	49
Jamie, Andrew (fl. 1678)	41
Jamie, Andrew (fl. 1790s)	6
Jamie, David (fl. 1721)	57
Jamie, David (fl. 1678)	41

J (cont.)

Jeamie, John (fl. 1751)	49
Jamie, John (fl. 1772)	66-68
Jeamie, Margaret	69-73
Jamie, Mary	73
Jeamie, William (fl. 1751)	49
Jamie, William in Hilsyd	13
Jamieson, Alexander	65
"Jean Ravel"	7
Johnshaven	12, 47

K

Keith, Rev. Alexander	38
Kemlo, Helen (Mrs Gowan)	37
Killing Times	41

L

Largie, Margaret	45
Law, Alexander, in Johnshaven	73
Law, David	41
Law, Robert	65
Legal History	63-74
Case-list	78-79
Livie, John, Baillie in Montrose	67
Lownie Family	75
Lownie, Andrew	28
Lownie, David	69
Lownie, Liz	12

M

"Mary Bang"	7
Massie, Arthur	64
McMaire, John	40
Meal Mob Riots	25, 69, 72-74
Mearns Family	9
Mearns, Andrew	9, 64
Meirnes (Mearns), David	9
Mearns, George	7
Meirnes (Mearns), Issobell	9
Mearns, John (fl. 1732)	45
Mearns, John (fl. 1656)	65
Mearns, Margaret	60
Mearns, Robert (fl. 1696)	10
Mearns, Robert (fl. 1751)	59
Mearns, Robert (Kirk Elder)	43-50, 57
Mearns, Robert (fl. 1755)	66
Mearns, Thomas (fl. 1656)	65
Mearns, Thomas (Kirk Elder)	43
Mearns, William	60
Mills, Thomas	33
Milne, George	36-37, 66
Milne, James (fl. 1778)	69
Milne, James (fl. 1732)	45
Milne, John	66

M (Cont.)

Moncur Family (note)	12, 39
Moncur, Rev. Andrew	39
Montrose	11, 16, 17, 42
Montrose Burgh Court	63
Moray, Earl of	38
Mowat Family	12
Mowat, James (from Kinneff)	25, 57, 60, 66
Mowat, John	60

N

Napier, Margaret	40
Napier, Robert	32, 72
Newton, David, in Montrose	16
Nicoll Family (note)	11
Nicoll, Margaret	14

P

"Protest" of 1676	41
"Protest" of 1714	43
Poor Roll 1648	56

R

Rait of Hallgreen Family	2, 24
Rait, David	3, 27
Rait, John	3, 9, 27
Rait, Rev. Peter	40-42
Rattray, David	39
Ritchie Family (alias Fatt)	10
Ritchie, Jon	11
Ritchie, Kathren	11
Ritchie, Thomas	11

S

Scott, Christian	45
Sharp, John	33
Ships – *Robert* of Gourdon	5
Ann of Gourdon	34
Isobel of Gourdon	68
Shore Inn	28
Sime, Walter	32
Slough of Despond	6
Smith, Adam	71
Smith, Alexander, in Maurdie	68
Smuggling	27-37
Spence Family	13-14
Spence, John	13
Spence, Margaret	13
St Monance Gowans	29
Storm of 1648	56
Storm of 1782	25
Storm of Wind	4, 25, 29
Stonehaven Sheriff Court	63

S (Cont.)

Strachan, James	32, 66, 71
Strachan, Rev. James	39
Sunderland	68
Symson, James	38

T

Taylor, Ann	74
Testificat System	49
Thom, Walter	1, 21, 37, 51, 75
Todd Family	9-10
Todd, David	9-10, 64
Trade	27-37
Trafalgar, Battle of	15

W

Walker, Robert	69
Walsh, Robert	46
Walsh, Robert, in Falside	66
Watt, Daniel	47
Watt, James	66-67
Watt, Jean (fl. 1755)	65
Watt, Jean (fl. 1732)	45
Watt, Robert	33
Werewolf Cairn	21
William of Orange	42
Wright, Rev. William	39
Wyse, David	65

Y

Yorkshire Connections	12